Sri Aurobindo

Rebirth and Karma

Publisher:
Lotus Light Publications
P.O. Box 2
Wilmot, WI 53192 USA

First published serially 1915 and 1919-21
Published in India under the title *The Problem of Rebirth*

First edition 1952
First American edition 1991

© Sri Aurobindo Ashram Trust 1952, 1991

This edition is published and distributed in the United States by
Lotus Light Publications, P. O. Box 2, Wilmot, WI 53192
by arrangement with Sri Aurobindo Ashram Trust
Publication Department, Pondicherry 605 002, India
ISBN 0-941524-63-9 Paper Bound

Library of Congress Catalogue Card Number 90-63095

Printed at the Sri Aurobindo Ashram Press
Pondicherry, India
PRINTED IN INDIA

Publisher's Note

The essays that make up this book were first published in the monthly review *Arya* in 1915 and 1919-21. Towards the end of the 1920s Sri Aurobindo revised them with the intention of bringing them out as a book and also wrote several drafts of a new essay or essays to be added to the others. He never completed this work, however, and it was not until 1952, two years after his passing, that the book was published. All the material in the present edition has been carefully checked against the relevant manuscripts and printed texts. Some typographical and other errors have been corrected.

CONTENTS

Section I
Rebirth and Karma

Section II
The Lines of Karma

SECTION ONE

REBIRTH AND KARMA

Rebirth

The theory of rebirth is almost as ancient as thought itself and its origin is unknown. We may according to our prepossessions accept it as the fruit of ancient psychological experience always renewable and verifiable and therefore true or dismiss it as a philosophical dogma and ingenious speculation; but in either case the doctrine, even as it is in all appearance well-nigh as old as human thought itself, is likely also to endure as long as human beings continue to think.

In former times the doctrine used to pass in Europe under the grotesque name of transmigration which brought with it to the Western mind the humorous image of the soul of Pythagoras migrating, a haphazard bird of passage, from the human form divine into the body of a guinea-pig or an ass. The philosophical appreciation of the theory expressed itself in the admirable but rather unmanageable Greek word, metempsychosis, which means the insouling of a new body by the same psychic individual. The Greek tongue is always happy in its marriage of thought and word and a better expression could not be found; but forced into English speech the word becomes merely long and pedantic without any memory of its subtle Greek sense and has to be abandoned. Reincarnation is the now popular term, but the idea in the word leans to the gross or external view of the fact and begs many questions. I prefer "rebirth," for it renders the sense of the wide, colourless, but sufficient Sanskrit term, *punarjanma*, "again-birth," and commits us to nothing but the fundamental idea which is the essence and life of the doctrine.

Rebirth is for the modern mind no more than a speculation and a theory; it has never been proved by the methods of modern science or to the satisfaction of the new critical mind formed by a scientific culture. Neither has it been disproved; for modern science knows nothing about a before-life or an after-life for the human soul, knows nothing indeed about a soul at all, nor can know; its province stops with the flesh and brain and nerve, the embryo and its formation and development. Neither has modern criticism any apparatus by which the truth or untruth of rebirth can be established. In fact, modern criticism, with all its pretensions to

searching investigation and scrupulous certainty, is no very efficient truth-finder. Outside the sphere of the immediate physical it
is almost helpless. It is good at discovering data, but except where
the data themselves bear on the surface their own conclusion, it
has no means of being rightly sure of the generalisations it
announces from them so confidently in one generation and
destroys in the next. It has no means of finding out with surety the
truth or untruth of a doubtful historical assertion; after a century
of dispute it has not even been able to tell us yes or no, whether
Jesus Christ ever existed. How then shall it deal with such a matter
as this of rebirth which is stuff of psychology and must be settled
rather by psychological than physical evidence?

The arguments which are usually put forward by supporters
and opponents, are often weak or futile and even at their best
insufficient either to prove or to disprove anything in the world.
One argument, for instance, often put forward triumphantly in
disproof is this that we have no memory of our past lives and
therefore there were no past lives! One smiles to see such
reasoning seriously used by those who imagine that they are
something more than intellectual children. The argument proceeds
on psychological grounds and yet it ignores the very nature of our
ordinary or physical memory which is all that the normal man can
employ. How much do we remember of our actual lives which we
are undoubtedly living at the present moment? Our memory is
normally good for what is near, becomes vaguer or less comprehensive as its objects recede into the distance, farther off seizes
only some salient points and, finally, for the beginning of our lives
falls into a mere blankness. Do we remember even the mere fact,
the simple state of being an infant on the mother's breast? and yet
that state of infancy was, on any but a Buddhist theory, part of the
same life and belonged to the same individual, — the very one who
cannot remember it just as he cannot remember his past lives. Yet
we demand that this physical memory, this memory of the brute
brain of man which cannot remember our infancy and has lost so
much of our later years, shall recall that which was before infancy,
before birth, before itself was formed. And if it cannot, we are to
cry, "Disproved your reincarnation theory!" The sapient insi-
piency of our ordinary human reasoning could go no farther than
in this sort of ratiocination. Obviously, if our past lives are to be
remembered whether as fact and state or in their events and

images, it can only be by a psychical memory awaking which will overcome the limits of the physical and resuscitate impressions other than those stamped on the physical being by physical cerebration.

I doubt whether, even if we could have evidence of the physical memory of past lives or of such a psychical awakening, the theory would be considered any better proved than before. We now hear of many such instances confidently alleged though without that apparatus of verified evidence responsibly examined which gives weight to the results of psychical research. The sceptic can always challenge them as mere fiction and imagination unless and until they are placed on a firm basis of evidence. Even if the facts alleged are verified, he has the resource of affirming that they are not really memories but were known to the person alleging them by ordinary physical means or were suggested to him by others and have been converted into reincarnate memory either by conscious deception or by a process of self-deception and self-hallucination. And even supposing the evidence were too strong and unexceptionable to be got rid of by these familiar devices, they might yet not be accepted as proof of rebirth; the mind can discover a hundred theoretical explanations for a single group of facts. Modern speculation and research have brought in this doubt to overhang all psychical theory and generalisation.

We know for instance that in the phenomena, say, of automatic writing or of communication from the dead, it is disputed whether the phenomena proceed from outside, from disembodied minds, or from within, from the subliminal consciousness, or whether the communication is actual and immediate from the released personality or is the uprising to the surface of a telepathic impression which came from the mind of the then living man but has remained submerged in our subliminal mentality. The same kind of doubts might be opposed to the evidences of reincarnate memory. It might be maintained that they prove the power of a certain mysterious faculty in us, a consciousness that can have some inexplicable knowledge of past events, but that these events may belong to other personalities than ours and that our attribution of them to our own personality in past lives is an imagination, a hallucination, or else an instance of that self-appropriation of things and experiences perceived but not our own which is one out of the undoubted phenomena of mental error. Much would be proved by an accumulation of such evidences but not, to the sceptic at least, rebirth. Certainly, if they were sufficiently ample, exact, profuse, intimate, they would create an atmosphere which would lead in the end to a general acceptance of the theory by the human race as a moral certitude. But proof is a different matter.

After all, most of the things that we accept as truths are really no more than moral certitudes. We have all the profoundest unshakeable faith that the earth revolves on its own axis, but as has been pointed out by a great French mathematician, the fact has never been proved; it is only a theory which accounts well for certain observable facts, no more. Who knows whether it may not be replaced in this or another century by a better—or a worse? All observed astronomical phenomena were admirably accounted for by theories of spheres and I know not what else, before Galileo came in with his "And yet it moves," disturbing the infallibility of Popes and Bibles and the science and logic of the learned. One feels certain that admirable theories could be invented to account for the facts of gravitation if our intellects were not prejudiced and prepossessed by the anterior demonstrations of Newton.[1] This is the ever-perplexing and inherent plague of our reason; for it starts by knowing nothing and has to deal with infinite possibilities, and the possible explanations of any given set of facts until we actually know what is behind them, are endless. In the end, we really know only what we observe and even that subject to a haunting question, for instance, that green is green and white is white, although it appears that colour is not colour but something else that creates the appearance of colour. Beyond observable fact we must be content with reasonable logical satisfaction, dominating probability and moral certitude,—at least until we have the sense to observe that there are faculties in us higher than the sense-dependent reason and awaiting development by which we can arrive at greater certainties.

We cannot really assert as against the sceptic any such dominant probability or any such certitude on behalf of the theory of rebirth. The external evidence yet available is in the last degree rudimentary. Pythagoras was one of the greatest of sages, but his assertion that he fought at Troy under the name of the Antenorid and was slain by the younger son of Atreus is an assertion only and his identification of the Trojan shield will convince no one who is

---

[1] This was written in pre-Einsteinian days.

not already convinced; the modern evidence is not as yet any more convincing than the proof of Pythagoras. In absence of external proof which to our matter-governed sensational intellects is alone conclusive, we have the argument of the reincarnationists that their theory accounts for all the facts better than any other yet advanced. The claim is just, but it does not create any kind of certitude. The theory of rebirth coupled with that of Karma gives us a simple, symmetrical, beautiful explanation of things; but so too the theory of the spheres gave us once a simple, symmetrical, beautiful explanation of the heavenly movements. Yet we have now got quite another explanation, much more complex, much more Gothic and shaky in its symmetry, an inexplicable order evolved out of chaotic infinities, which we accept[1] as the truth of the matter. And yet, if we will only think, we shall perhaps see that even this is not the whole truth; there is much more behind we have not yet discovered. Therefore the simplicity, symmetry, beauty, satisfactoriness of the reincarnation theory is no warrant of its certitude.

When we go into details, the uncertainty increases. Rebirth accounts, for example, for the phenomenon of genius, inborn faculty and so many other psychological mysteries. But then Science comes in with its all-sufficient explanation by heredity, —though, like that of rebirth, all-sufficient only to those who already believe in it. Without doubt, the claims of heredity have been absurdly exaggerated. It has succeeded in accounting for much, not all, in our physical make-up, our temperament, our vital peculiarities. Its attempt to account for genius, inborn faculty and other psychological phenomena of a higher kind is a pretentious failure. But this may be because Science knows nothing at all that is fundamental about our psychology, —no more than primitive astronomers knew of the constitution and law of the stars whose movements they yet observed with a sufficient accuracy. I do not think that even when Science knows more and better, it will be able to explain these things by heredity; but the scientist may well argue that he is only at the beginning of his researches, that the generalisation which has explained so much may well explain

[1] Or used to accept, but now it is suggested that this order is only a schema created by our own mind or determined by the constitution of our brain, a syntax and logic of word and thought which we impose on a world that in fact does not or may not contain any such thing.

all, and that at any rate his hypothesis has had a better start in its
equipment of provable facts than the theory of reincarnation.

Nevertheless, the argument of the reincarnationist is so far a
good argument and respect-worthy, though not conclusive. But
there is another more clamorously advanced which seems to me to
be on a par with the hostile reasoning from absence of memory, at
least in the form in which it is usually advanced to attract unripe
minds. This is the ethical argument by which it is sought to justify
God's ways with the world or the world's ways with itself. There
must, it is thought, be a moral governance for the world; or at least
some sanction of reward in the cosmos for virtue, some sanction of
punishment for sin. But upon our perplexed and chaotic earth no
such sanction appears. We see the good man thrust down into the
press of miseries and the wicked flourishing like a green bay-tree
and *not* cut down miserably in his end. Now this is intolerable. It is
a cruel anomaly, it is a reflection on God's wisdom and justice,
almost a proof that God is not; we must remedy that. Or if God is
not, we must have some other sanction for righteousness.

How comforting it would be if we could tell a good man and
even the amount of his goodness, — for should not the Supreme be
a strict and honourable accountant? — by the amount of ghee that
he is allowed to put into his stomach and the number of rupees he
can jingle into his bank and the various kinds of good luck that
accrue to him. Yes, and how comforting too if we could point our
finger at the wicked stripped of all concealment and cry at him, "O
thou wicked one! for if thou wert not evil, wouldst thou in a world
governed by God or at least by good, be thus ragged, hungry,
unfortunate, pursued by griefs, void of honour among men? Yes,
thou art proved wicked, because thou art ragged. God's justice is
established." The Supreme Intelligence being fortunately wiser
and nobler than man's childishness, this is impossible. But let us
take comfort! It appears that if the good man has not enough good
luck and ghee and rupees, it is because he is really a scoundrel
suffering for his crimes, — but a scoundrel in his past life who has
suddenly turned a new leaf in his mother's womb; and if yonder
wicked man flourishes and tramples gloriously on the world, it is
because of his goodness — in a past life, the saint that was then
having since been converted — was it by his experience of the
temporal vanity of virtue? — to the cult of sin. All is explained, all
is justified. We suffer for our sins in another body; we shall be

rewarded in another body for our virtues in this; and so it will go on *ad infinitum*. No wonder, the philosophers found this a bad business and proposed as a remedy to get rid of both sin and virtue and even as our highest good to scramble anyhow out of a world so amazingly governed.

Obviously, this scheme of things is only a variation of the old spiritual-material bribe and menace, the bribe of a Heaven of fat joys for the good and the threat of a hell of eternal fire or bestial tortures for the wicked. The idea of the Law of the world as primarily a dispenser of rewards and punishments is cognate to the idea of the Supreme Being as a judge, "father" and school-master who is continually rewarding with lollipops his good boys and continually caning his naughty urchins. It is cognate also to the barbarous and unthinking system of sometimes savage and always degrading punishment for social offences on which human society, unable still to find out or organise a more satisfactory way, is still founded. Man insists continually on making God in his own image instead of seeking to make himself more and more in the image of God, and all these ideas are the reflection of the child and the savage and the animal in us which we have still failed to transform or outgrow. We should be inclined to wonder how these fancies of children found their way into such profound philosophical religions as Buddhism and Hinduism, if it were not so patent that men will not deny themselves the luxury of tacking on the rubbish from their past to the deeper thoughts of their sages.

No doubt, since these ideas were so prominent, they must have had their use in training humanity. Perhaps even it is true that the Supreme deals with the child soul according to its childishness and allows it to continue its sensational imaginations of heaven and hell for a time beyond the death of the physical body. Perhaps both these ideas of after-life and of rebirth as fields of punishment and reward were needed because suited to our half-mentalised animality. But after a certain stage the system ceases to be really effective. Men believe in Heaven and Hell but go on sinning merrily, quit at last by a Papal indulgence or the final priestly absolution or a death-bed repentance or a bath in the Ganges or a sanctified death at Benares, — such are the childish devices by which we escape from our childishness! And in the end the mind grows adult and puts the whole nursery nonsense away with contempt. The reward and punishment theory of rebirth, if a

little more elevated or at least less crudely sensational, comes to be
as ineffective. And it is good that it should be so. For it is
intolerable that man with his divine capacity should continue to be
virtuous for a reward and shun sin out of terror. Better a strong
sinner than a selfish virtuous coward or a petty huckster with God;
there is more divinity in him, more capacity of elevation. Truly the
Gita has said well, *kṛpaṇāḥ phalahetavaḥ*. And it is inconceivable
that the system of this vast and majestic world should have been
founded on these petty and paltry motives. There is reason in
these theories? then reason of the nursery, puerile. Ethics? then
ethics of the mud, muddy.

The true foundation of the theory of rebirth is the evolution of
the soul, or rather its efflorescence out of the veil of Matter and its
gradual self-finding. Buddhism contained this truth involved in its
theory of Karma and emergence out of Karma but failed to bring it
to light; Hinduism knew it of old, but afterwards missed the right
balance of its expression. Now we are again able to restate the
ancient truth in a new language and this is already being done by
certain schools of thought, though still the old incrustations tend to
tack themselves on to the deeper wisdom. And if this gradual
efflorescence be true, then the theory of rebirth is an intellectual
necessity, a logically unavoidable corollary. But what is the aim of
that evolution? Not conventional or interested virtue and the
faultless counting out of the small coin of good in the hope of an
apportioned material reward, but the continual growth towards a
divine knowledge, strength, love and purity. These things alone
are real virtue and this virtue is its own reward. The one true
reward of the works of love is to grow ever in capacity and delight
of love up to the ecstasy of the spirit's all-seizing embrace and
universal passion; the one reward of the works of right Knowledge
is to grow perpetually into the infinite Light; the one reward of the
works of right Power is to harbour more and more of the Force
Divine, and of the works of purity to be freed more and more from
egoism into that immaculate wideness where all things are transformed and reconciled into the divine equality. To seek other
reward is to bind oneself to a foolishness and a childish ignorance;
and to regard even these things as a reward is an unripeness and an
imperfection.

And what of suffering and happiness, misfortune and prosperity? These are experiences of the soul in its training, helps,

props, means, disciplines, tests, ordeals, — and prosperity often a worse ordeal than suffering. Indeed, adversity, suffering may often be regarded rather as a reward to virtue than as a punishment for sin, since it turns out to be the greatest help and purifier of the soul struggling to unfold itself. To regard it merely as the stern award of a Judge, the anger of an irritated Ruler or even the mechanical recoil of result of evil upon cause of evil is to take the most superficial view possible of God's dealings with the soul and the law of the world's evolution. And what of worldly prosperity, wealth, progeny, the outward enjoyment of art, beauty, power? Good, if they be achieved without loss to the soul and enjoyed only as the outflowing of the divine Joy and Grace upon our material existence. But let us seek them first for others or rather for all, and for ourselves only as a part of the universal condition or as one means of bringing perfection nearer.

The soul needs no proof of its rebirth any more than it needs proof of its immortality. For there comes a time when it is consciously immortal, aware of itself in its eternal and immutable essence. Once that realisation is accomplished, all intellectual questionings for and against the immortality of the soul fall away like a vain clamour of ignorance around the self-evident and ever-present truth. *Tato na vicikitsate*. That is the true dynamic belief in immortality when it becomes to us not an intellectual dogma but a fact as evident as the physical fact of our breathing and as little in need of proof or argument. So also there comes a time when the soul becomes aware of itself in its eternal and mutable movement; it is then aware of the ages behind that constituted the present organisation of the movement, sees how this was prepared in an uninterrupted past, remembers something of the bygone soul-states, environments, particular forms of activity which built up its present constituents and knows to what it is moving by development in an uninterrupted future. This is the true dynamic belief in rebirth, and there too the play of the questioning intellect ceases; the soul's vision and the soul's memory are all. Certainly, there remains the question of the mechanism of the development and of the laws of rebirth where the intellect and its inquiries and generalisations can still have some play. And here the more one thinks and experiences, the more the ordinary, simple, cut-and-dried account of reincarnation seems to be of doubtful validity. There is surely here a greater complexity, a law evolved with a more difficult movement and a more intricate harmony out of the possibilities of the Infinite. But this is a question which demands long and ample consideration; for subtle is the law of it. *Aṇur hyeṣa dharmaḥ*.

The Reincarnating Soul

Human thought in the generality of men is no more than a rough and crude acceptance of unexamined ideas. Our mind is a sleepy or careless sentry and allows anything to pass the gates which seems to it decently garbed or wears a plausible appearance or can mumble anything that resembles some familiar password. Especially is this so in subtle matters, those remote from the concrete facts of our physical life and environment. Even men who will reason carefully and acutely in ordinary matters and there consider vigilance against error an intellectual or a practical duty, are yet content with the most careless stumbling when they get upon higher and more difficult ground. Where precision and subtle thinking are most needed, there they are most impatient of it and averse to the labour demanded of them. Men can manage fine thought about palpable things, but to think subtly about the subtle is too great a strain on the grossness of our intellects; so we are content with making a dab at the truth, like the painter who threw his brush at his picture when he could not get the effect that he desired. We mistake the smudge that results for the perfect form of a verity.

It is not surprising then that men should be content to think crudely about such a matter as rebirth. Those who accept it, take it usually ready made, either as a cut and dried theory or a crude dogma. The soul is reborn in a new body, — that vague and almost meaningless assertion is for them sufficient. But what is the soul and what can possibly be meant by the rebirth of a soul? Well, it means reincarnation; the soul, whatever that may be, had got out of one case of flesh and is now getting into another case of flesh. It sounds simple, — let us say, like the Djinn of the Arabian tale expanding out of and again compressing himself into his bottle or perhaps as a pillow is lugged out of one pillow-case and thrust into another. Or the soul fashions for itself a body in the mother's womb and then occupies it, or else, let us say, puts off one robe of flesh and then puts on another. But what is it that thus "leaves" one body and "enters" into another? Is it another, a psychic body and subtle form, that enters into the gross corporeal form, — the Purusha perhaps of the ancient image, no bigger than a man's thumb, or is it something in itself formless and impalpable that incarnates in the sense of becoming or assuming to the senses a palpable shape of bone and flesh?

In the ordinary, the vulgar conception there is no birth of a soul at all, but only the birth of a new body into the world occupied by an old personality unchanged from that which once left some now discarded physical frame. It is John Robinson who has gone out of the form of flesh he once occupied; it is John Robinson who tomorrow or some centuries hence will re-incarnate in another form of flesh and resume the course of his terrestrial experiences with another name and in another environment. Achilles, let us say, is reborn as Alexander, the son of Philip, a Macedonian, conqueror not of Hector but of Darius, with a wider scope, with larger destinies; but it is still Achilles, it is the same personality that is reborn, only the bodily circumstances are different. It is this survival of the identical personality that attracts the European mind today in the theory of reincarnation. For it is the extinction or dissolution of the personality, of this mental, nervous and physical composite which I call myself that is hard to bear for the man enamoured of life, and it is the promise of its survival and physical reappearance that is the great lure. The one objection that really stands in the way of its acceptance is the obvious non-survival of memory. Memory is the man, says the modern psychologist, and what is the use of the survival of my personality, if I do not remember my past, if I am not aware of being the same person still and always? What is the utility? Where is the enjoyment?

The old Indian thinkers, — I am not speaking of the popular belief which was crude enough and thought not at all about the matter, — the old Buddhistic and Vedantist thinkers surveyed the whole field from a very different standpoint. They were not attached to the survival of the personality; they did not give to that survival the high name of immortality; they saw that personality being what it is, a constantly changing composite, the survival of an identical personality was a non-sense, a contradiction in terms. They perceived indeed that there is a continuity and they sought to discover what determines this continuity and whether the sense of identity which enters into it is an illusion or the representation of a fact, of a real truth, and, if the latter, then what that truth may be. The Buddhist denied any real identity. There is, he said, no self, no person; there is simply a continuous stream of energy in action like the continuous flowing of a river or the continuous burning of a flame. It is this continuity which creates in the mind the false sense of identity. I am not now the same person that I was a year ago, not even the same person that I was a moment ago, any more than the water flowing past yonder ghaut is the same water that flowed past it a few seconds ago; it is the persistence of the flow in the same channel that preserves the false appearance of identity. Obviously, then, there is no soul that reincarnates, but only Karma that persists in flowing continuously down an apparently uninterrupted channel. It is Karma that incarnates; Karma creates the form of a constantly changing mentality and physical bodies that are, we may presume, the result of that changing composite of ideas and sensations which I call myself. The identical "I" is not, never was, never will be. Practically, so long as the error of personality persists, this does not make much difference and I can say in the language of ignorance that I am reborn in a new body; practically, I have to proceed on the basis of that error. But there is this important point gained that it is all an error and an error which can cease; the composite can be broken up for good without any fresh formation, the flame can be extinguished, the channel which called itself a river destroyed. And then there is non-being, there is cessation, there is the release of the error from itself.

The Vedantist comes to a different conclusion; he admits an identical, a self, a persistent immutable reality, — but other than my personality, other than this composite which I call myself. In the Katha Upanishad the question is raised in a very instructive fashion quite apposite to the subject we have in hand. Nachiketas, sent by his father to the world of Death, thus questions Yama, the lord of that world: Of the man who has gone forward, who has passed away from us, some say that he is and others "this he is not"; which then is right? what is the truth of the great passage? Such is the form of the question and at first sight it seems simply to raise the problem of immortality in the European sense of the word, the survival of the identical personality. But that is not what Nachiketas asks. He has already taken as the second of three boons offered to him by Yama the knowledge of the sacred Flame by which man crosses over hunger and thirst, leaves sorrow and fear far behind him and dwells in heaven securely rejoicing. Immortality in that sense he takes for granted as, already standing in that farther world, he must surely do. The knowledge he asks for involves the deeper, finer problem, of which Yama affirms that even the gods debated this of old and it is not easy to know, for subtle is the law of it; something survives that appears to be the same person, that descends into hell, that ascends into heaven, that returns upon the earth with a new body, but is it really the same person that thus survives? Can we really say of the man "*He* still is," or must we not rather say "This *he* no longer is"? Yama too in his answer speaks not at all of the survival of death, and he only gives a verse or two to a bare description of that constant rebirth which all serious thinkers admitted as a universally acknowledged truth. What he speaks of is the Self, the real Man, the Lord of all these changing appearances; without the knowledge of that Self the survival of the personality is not immortal life but a constant passing from death to death; he only who goes beyond personality to the real Person becomes the Immortal. Till then a man seems indeed to be born again and again by the force of his knowledge and works, name succeeds to name, form gives place to form, but there is no immortality.

Such then is the real question put and answered so divergently by the Buddhist and the Vedantin. There is a constant reforming of personality in new bodies, but this personality is a mutable creation of force at its work streaming forward in Time and never for a moment the same, and the ego-sense that makes us cling to the life of the body and believe readily that it is the same idea and form, that it is John Robinson who is reborn as Sidi Hossain, is a creation of the mentality. Achilles was not reborn as Alexander, but the stream of force in its works which created the momentarily changing mind and body of Achilles flowed on and created the momentarily changing mind and body of Alexander. Still, said the ancient Vedanta, there is yet something beyond this force in action, Master of it, one who makes it create for him new names and forms, and that is the Self, the Purusha, the Man, the Real Person. The ego-sense is only its distorted image reflected in the flowing stream of embodied mentality.

Is it then the Self that incarnates and reincarnates? But the Self is imperishable, immutable, unborn, undying. The Self is not born and does not exist in the body; rather the body is born and exists in the Self. For the Self is one everywhere,—*in* all bodies, we say, but really it is not confined and parcelled out in different bodies except as the all-constituting ether seems to be formed into different objects and is in a sense in them. Rather all these bodies are in the Self; but that also is a figment of space-conception, and rather these bodies are only symbols and figures of itself created by it in its own consciousness. Even what we call the individual soul is greater than its body and not less, more subtle than it and therefore not confined by its grossness. At death it does not leave its form, but casts it off, so that a great departing Soul can say of this death in vigorous phrase, "I have spat out the body."

What then is it that we feel to inhabit the physical frame? What is it that the Soul draws out from the body when it casts off this partial physical robe which enveloped not it, but part of its members? What is it whose issuing out gives this wrench, this swift struggle and pain of parting, creates this sense of violent divorce? The answer does not help us much. It is the subtle or psychical frame which is tied to the physical by the heart-strings, by the cords of life-force, of nervous energy which have been woven into every physical fibre. This the Lord of the body draws out and the violent snapping or the rapid or tardy loosening of the life-chords, the exit of the connecting force constitutes the pain of death and its difficulty.

Let us then change the form of the question and ask rather what it is that reflects and accepts the mutable personality, since the Self is immutable? We have in fact an immutable Self, a real Person, lord of this ever-changing personality which, again, assumes ever-changing bodies, but the real Self knows itself always as above the mutation, watches and enjoys it, but is not involved in it. Through what does it enjoy the changes and feel them to be its own, even while knowing itself to be unaffected by them? The mind and ego-sense are only inferior instruments; there must be some more essential form of itself which the Real Man puts forth, puts in front of itself, as it were, and at the back of the changings to support and mirror them without being actually changed by them. This more essential form is or seems to be in man the mental being or mental person which the Upanishads speak of as the mental leader of the life and body, *manomayaḥ prāṇa-śarīra-netā*. It is that which maintains the ego-sense as a function in the mind and enables us to have the firm conception of continuous identity in Time as opposed to the timeless identity of the Self.

The changing personality is not this mental person; it is a

composite of various stuff of Nature, a formation of Prakriti and is not at all the Purusha. And it is a very complex composite with many layers; there is a layer of physical, a layer of nervous, a layer of mental, even a final stratum of supramental personality; and within these layers themselves there are strata within each stratum. The analysis of the successive couches of the earth is a simple matter compared with the analysis of this wonderful creation we call the personality. The mental being in resuming bodily life forms a new personality for its new terrestrial existence; it takes material from the common matter-stuff, life-stuff, mind-stuff of the physical world and during earthly life it is constantly absorbing fresh material, throwing out what is used up, changing its bodily, nervous and mental tissues. But this is all surface work; behind is the foundation of past experience held back from the physical memory so that the superficial consciousness may not be troubled or interfered with by the conscious burden of the past but may concentrate on the work immediately in hand. Still that foundation of past experience is the bed-rock of personality; and it is more than that. It is our real fund on which we can always draw even apart from our present superficial commerce with our surroundings. That commerce adds to our gains, modifies the foundation for a subsequent existence.

Moreover, all this is, again, on the surface. It is only a small part of ourselves which lives and acts in the energies of our earthly existence. As behind the physical universe there are worlds of which ours is only a last result, so also within us there are worlds of our self-existence which throw out this external form of our being. The subconscient, the super-conscient are oceans from which and to which this river flows. Therefore to speak of ourselves as a soul reincarnating is to give altogether too simple an appearance to the miracle of our existence; it puts into too ready and too gross a formula the magic of the supreme Magician. There is not a definite psychic entity getting into a new case of flesh; there is a metempsychosis, a reinsouling, a rebirth of new psychic personality as well as a birth of a new body. And behind is the Person, the unchanging entity, the Master who manipulates this complex material, the Artificer of this wondrous artifice.

This is the starting-point from which we have to proceed in considering the problem of rebirth. To view ourselves as such and such a personality getting into a new case of flesh is to stumble about in the ignorance, to confirm the error of the material mind and the senses. The body is a convenience, the personality is a constant formation for whose development action and experience are the instruments; but the Self by whose will and for whose delight all this is, is other than the body, other than the action and experience, other than the personality which they develop. To ignore it is to ignore the whole secret of our being.

Rebirth, Evolution, Heredity

Two truths, discoveries with an enormous periphery of luminous result and of a considerable essential magnitude, evolution and heredity, figure to-day in the front of thought, and I suppose we have to take them as a well-established unquenchable light upon our being, lamps of a constant lustre, though not yet very perfectly trimmed, final so far as anything is final in man's constantly changing cinematographic process of the development of intellectual knowledge. They may be said to make up almost the whole fundamental idea of life in the way of seeing peculiar to a mind dominated, fashioned, pressed into its powerful moulds by the exact, curious, multifariously searching, yet in the end singularly limited observation and singularly narrow reason of our modern science. Science is in her own way a great seer and magician; she has both the microscopic and the macroscopic, the closely gazing and the telescopic view, a dissolving power of searching analytic resolution, a creative power of revealing synthetic effectuation. She has hunted to their lair many of the intermediate secret processes of the great creatrix, and even she has been able, by the inventive faculty given to us, to go and do one better. Man, this midget in infinity, locomotive yet nailed to the contiguity of a petty crust of soil by the force of gravitation, has certainly scored by her a goodly number of points against the mother of the universe. But all this has been done in some perfection only in the limits of her lowest obtrusive physical field.

Face to face with psychic and spiritual secrecies, as in the open elementary world even of mind, Science has still the uninformed gaze and the groping hands of the infant. In that sphere she, so precise, illuminative, compelling in the physical, sees only the big blazing buzzing confusion which James tells us, with a possibly inaccurate vividness of alliterative phrase, is the newborn baby's view of the sensible world into which he has dropped down the mysterious stairs of birth. Science, faced with what are still to her the wonderful random accords and unexplained miracles of consciousness, protects herself from the errors of the imagination,—but stumbling incidentally by that very fact into plenty of the errors of an inadequate induction,—behind an opaque shield of cautelous scepticism. She clings with the grasping firmness of the half-drowned to planks of security she thinks she has got in a few well-tested correspondences, — so-styled, though the word as used explains nothing, — between mental action and its accompaniment of suggestive or instrumental physical functionings. She is determined, if she can, to explain every supraphysical phenomenon by some physical fact; psychological process of mind must not exist except as result or rendering of physiological process of body. This set resolution, apparently rational and cautious of ascertainable and firmly tangible truth, but really heroic in its paradoxical temerity, shuts up her chance of rapid discovery, for the present at least, in a fairly narrow circle. It taints too her extensions of physical truth into the psychological field with a pursuing sense of inadequacy. And this inadequacy in extended application is very evident in her theories of heredity and evolution when she forces them beyond their safe ground of physical truth and labours to illumine by them the subtle, complex, elusive phenomena of our psychological being.

There are still, I dare say, persons here and there who cherish a secret or an open unfaith in the theory of a physical evolution and believe that it will one day pass into the limbo of dead generalisations like the Ptolemaic theory in astronomy or like the theory of humours in medicine; but this is a rare and excessive scepticism. Yet it may not be without use or aptitude for our purpose to note that contrary to current popular notions the scientific account of this generalisation, like that of a good number of others, is not yet conclusively proved, even though now taken for granted. But still there is on the whole a mass of facts and indications in its favour so considerable as to look overwhelming, so that we cannot resist the conclusion that in this way or some such way the whole thing came about and we find it difficult to conceive any more convincing explanation of the indubitable ascending and branching scale of genus and species which meets even our casual scrutiny of living existence. One thing at least seems now intellectually certain, we can no longer believe that these suns and systems were hurled full-shaped and eternally arranged into boundless space and all these numberless species of being planted on earth ready-made and nicely tailored in seven days or any number of days in a sudden outburst of caprice or Dionysiac excitement or crowded activity of mechanical conception by the fiat of a timeless Creator. The successive development which was summarily proposed by the ancient Hindu thinkers, the lower forms of being first, man afterwards as the crown of the Spirit's development of life on earth, has been confirmed by the patient and detailed scrutiny of physical science,— an aeonic development, though the farther Hindu conception of a constant repetition of the principle in cycles is necessarily incapable of physical evidence.

One thing more seems now equally certain that not only the seed of all life was one,— again the great intuition of the Upanishads foreruns the conclusions of the physical enquiry, one seed which the universal self-existence by process of force has disposed in many ways, *ekaṁ bījaṁ bahudhā śakti-yogāt*,— but even the principle of development is one and the structural ground-plan too as it develops step by step, in spite of all departures to this side or that in the workings of the creative Force or the creative Idea. Nature seems to start with an extraordinary poverty of original broad variative conceptions and to proceed to an extraordinary richness of her minuter consequential variations, which amounts to a forging of constant subtle differentiations of species and in the individual a startling insistence on result of uniqueness. It almost looks as if in the process of her physical harmonies there was meant to be some formal effect or symbolic reproduction of the truth that all things are originally one being, but a one who insists on his own infinite diversity, and even a suggestion that there is in this eternal unity an eternal pluralism, the Infinite Being self-repeated in an infinite multiplicity of beings each unique and yet each the One. To a mind on the look-out for the metaphysical suggestions we can draw from the apparent facts of being, that might not seem altogether an imagination.

In any case we have this now patent order in the profuse complexities of the natural harmony of living things,— one plasmic seed, one developing ground-plan, an opulent number of varieties whose logical process would be by an ascending order which passes up through fine but still very distinct gradations from the crude to the complex, from the less organised to the more organised, from the inferior to the superior type. The first question that should strike the mind at once, when this tree of life has been seen, is whether this logical order was indeed the actual order in the history of the universe, and then, a second, naturally arising from that problem, whether, if so, each new form developed by variation from its natural predecessor or came in by some unknown process, a fresh, independent and in a way sudden creation. In the first case, we have the scientific order of physical evolution,—in the other one knows not well what, perhaps an unseen Demiurge who developed the whole thing in the earlier period of the earth evolution and has now wholly or almost entirely stopped the business so that we have no new physical development of that kind, but only, it may be, an evolution of capacity in types already created. Science stands out for a quite natural and mechanical, a quite unbroken physical evolution with many divergent lines indeed of developing variation, but in the line no gap or interstice. It is true that there are not one but a host of missing links, which even the richest remains of the past cannot fill in, and we are not in a position to deny with an absolute dogmatism the possibility of an advance *per saltum*, by a rapid overleaping, perhaps even by a crowded psychical or bio-psychic preparation whose result sprang out in the appearance of a new type with a certain gulf between itself and the preceding forms of life. With regard to man especially there is still an enormous uncertainty as to how he, so like yet so different from the other sons of Nature, came into existence. Still the gaps can be explained away, there is a great mass of telling facts in favour of the less physically anarchic view, and it seems to have on its side the right of greatest probability in a material universe where the most perfectly physical principle of proceeding would seem to be the just basic law.

But even if we admit the most scrupulous and rigorous continuity of successive determination, the question arises whether the process of evolution has been indeed so exclusively physical and biological as at first sight it looks. If it is, we must admit not only a rigorous principle of class heredity, but a law of hereditary progressive variation and a purely physical cause of all mental and spiritual phenomena. Heredity by itself means simply the constant transmission of physical form and biological characteristics from a previous life to its posterity. There is very evidently such a general force of hereditary transmission within the genus or species itself, as the tree so the seed, as the seed so the tree, so that a lion generates a lion and not a cat or a rhinoceros, a man a human being and not an ourangoutang,—though one reads now of a curious and startling speculation, turning the old theory topsy-turvy, that certain ape kinds may be, not ancestors, but degenerate descendants of man! But farther, if a physical evolution is the whole fact, there must be a capacity for the hereditary transmission of variations by which new species are or have been created, — not merely in the process of a mixture or crossing, but by an internal development which is stored up and handed down in the seed. That too may very well be admitted, even though its real process and rationale are not yet understood, since the transmission of family and individual characteristics is a well observed phenomenon. But then the things transmitted are not only physical and biological, but psychological or at least bio-psychic characters, repetitions of customary nervous experience and mental tendency, powers. We have to suppose that the physical seed transmits these things. We are called upon to admit that the human seed for instance, which does not contain a developed human consciousness, yet carries with it the powers of such a consciousness so that they reproduce themselves automatically in the thinking and organised mentality of the offspring. This, even if we have to accept it, is an inexplicable paradox unless we suppose either that there is something more behind, a psychical power behind the veil of material process, or else that mind is only a process of life and life only a process of matter. Therefore finally we have to suppose the physical theory capable of explaining by purely material causes and a material constitution the mystery of the emergence of life in matter and the equal mystery of the emergence of mind in life. It is here that difficulties begin to crowd in which convict it, so far at least, of a hopeless inadequacy, and the nature of that inadequacy, its crux, its stumbling-point leave room for just that something behind, something psychical, a hidden soul process and for a more complex and less materialistic account of the truth of evolution.

The materialistic assumption—it is no more than a hypothetical assumption, for it has never been proved—is that development of non-living matter results under certain unknown conditions in a phenomenon of unconscious life which is in its real nature only an action and reaction of material energy, and the development of that again under certain unknown conditions in a phenomenon of conscious mind which is again in its real nature only an action and reaction of material energy. The thing is not proved, but that, it is argued, does not matter; it only means that we do not yet know enough; but one day we shall know, — the necessary physiological reaction called by us an intuition or train of reasoning crowned by discovery having, I suppose, taken place in a properly constituted nervous body and the more richly convoluted brain of a Galileo of biology, — and then this great and simple truth will be proved, like many other things once scoffed at by the shallow common sense of humanity. But the difficulty is that it seems incapable of proof. Even with regard to life, which is by a great deal the lesser difficulty, the discovery of certain chemical or other physical and mechanical conditions under which life can be stimulated to appear, will prove no more than that these are the favourable or necessary conditions for the manifestation of life in body, — such conditions there must be in the nature of things, — but not that life is not another new and higher power of the force of universal being. The connection of life responses with physical conditions and stimuli proves very clearly that life and matter are connected and that, as indeed they must do to coexist, the two kinds of energy act on each other, — a very ancient knowledge; but it does not get rid of the fact that the physical response is accompanied by an element which seems to be of the nature of a nervous excitement and an incipient or suppressed consciousness and is not the same thing as the companion physical reaction.

When we come to mind, we see — how could it be otherwise in an embodied mind? — a response, interaction, connection, a correspondence if you will; but no amount of correspondence can show how a physical response can be converted into or amount to or by itself constitute in result a conscious operation, a perception, emotion, thought-concept, or prove that love is a chemical product or that Plato's theory of ideas or Homer's Iliad or the cosmic consciousness of the Yogin was only a combination of physiological reactions or a complex of the changes of grey brain matter or a flaming marvel of electrical discharges. It is not only that common sense and imagination boggle at these theories, — that objection may be disregarded, — not only that perception, reason and intuition have to be thrust aside in favour of a forced and too extended inference, but that there is a gulf of difference here between the thing to be explained and the thing by which it is sought to explain it which cannot be filled up, however much we may admit nervous connections and psycho-physical bridges. And if the physical scientist points to a number of indicative facts and hopes one day to triumph over these formidable difficulties, there is growing up on the other side an incipient mass of psychical phenomena which are likely to drown his theory in fathomless waters. The insuperability of these always evident objections is beginning to be more widely recognised, but since the past still holds considerable sway, it is necessary to insist on them so that we may have the clear right to go on to more liberal hypotheses which do not try prematurely to reduce to a mechanical simplicity the problem of our being.

One of these is the ancient view that not only incidence of body and life on mind and soul, but incidence of mind and soul on body and life have to be considered. Here too there is the evolutionary idea, but physical and life evolution, even the growth of mind, are held to be only incidental to a soul evolution of which Time is the course and the earth among many other worlds the theatre. In the old Indian version of this theory evolution, heredity and rebirth are three companion processes of the universal unfolding, evolution the processional aim, rebirth the main method, heredity one of the physical conditions. That is a theory which provides at least the framework for a harmonious explanation of all the complex elements of the problem. The scientific idea starts from physical being and makes the psychical a result and circumstance of body; this other evolutionary idea starts from soul and sees in the physical being an instrumentation for the awakening to itself of a spirit absorbed in the universe of Matter.

Rebirth and Soul Evolution

The ideas that men currently form about life and things are for the most part pragmatic constructions. They are forms of a reason which is concerned with giving only such a serviceable account to itself of its surroundings as shall make a sufficient clue to our immediate business of the growth, action, satisfaction of the personality, something feasible, livable, effective for our journeying in Time, something viable, in the twofold French sense of the word. Whether it corresponds to or is directly in touch with any real reality of things seems to be very much a matter of accident. It seems to be sufficient if we can persuade our facile and complaisant reason of its truth and find it serviceable and fruitful in consequences for thought, action and life-experience. It is true that there is another unpragmatic reason in us which labours to get rid of this demand of the intellectual and vital personality; it wants to look at the real truth of things without veils and without any object, to mirror the very image of Truth in the still waters of a dispassionate, clear and pure mentality. But the workings of this calmer greater reason are hampered by two tremendous difficulties. First, it seems next to impossible to disengage it entirely from the rest of ourselves, from the normal intellectuality, from the will to believe, from that instinct of the intelligence which helps the survival, by a sort of subtle principle of preference and selection, of the way of thinking that suits our personal bent or the accomplished frame of our nature. And again, what is the Truth that our reason mirrors? It is after all some indirect image of Truth, not her very self and body seen face to face; it is an image moulded from such data, symbol, process of Reality, — if any real Reality there is, — as we can gather from the very limited experience of self and existing things open to human mind. So that unless there be some means by which knowledge can burst through all veils to the experience of the very Reality itself, or unless there be some universal Logos, divine Mind or Supermind, which knows itself and all things and our consciousness can reflect or get into touch with that, a pursuing insufficiency and uncertainty must always keep its baffling grasp upon even the highest power and largest walk of our reason and beset all the labour of human knowledge.

Nowhere are these disabilities more embarrassing than in those fundamental questions of the nature of the world and of our own existence which yet most passionately interest thinking humanity because this is in the end the thing of utmost importance to us, since everything else, except some rough immediate practicality of the moment, depends on its solution. And even that, until this great question is settled, is only a stumbling forward upon a journey of which we know not the goal or the purpose, the meaning or the necessity. The religions profess to solve these grand problems with an inspired or revealed certainty; but the enormity of their differences shows that in them too there is a selection of ideas, separate aspects of the Truth, — the sceptic would say, shows of imagination and falsehood, — and a construction from a limited spiritual experience. In them too there is an element of chosen and willed believing and some high pragmatic aim and utility, whether that be the soul's escape from the sorrow or unreality of existence or celestial bliss or a religio-ethical sanction and guidance. The philosophical systems are very obviously only feasible selective constructions of great reflective ideas. More often these are possibilities of the reason much rather than assured certainties or, if founded on spiritual experience, they are still selective constructions, a sort of great architectural approach to some gate into unknowable Divine or ineffable Infinite. The modern scientific mind professed to rid us of all mere intellectual constructions and put us face to face with truth and with assured truth only; it claimed the right to rid man of the fantastic encumbrance of religion and the nebulous futilities of metaphysical philosophy. But religion and philosophy have now turned upon science and convicted her, on her own statement of facts, of an equal liability to the two universal difficulties of human reason. The system of science seems to be itself only another feasible and fruitful construction of the reason giving a serviceable account to itself of the physical world and our relations to it, and it seems to be nothing more. And its knowledge is fatally bound by the limitation of its data and its outlook. Science too creates only a partial image of Truth stamped with a character of much uncertainty and still more clearly imprinted with the perverse hallmark of insufficiency.

We have to recognise that human reason, moving as it does from a starting-point of ignorance and in a great environing circle of ignorance, must proceed by hypothesis, assumption and theory subject to verification of some kind convincing to our reason and experience. But there is this difference that the religious mind accepts the theory or assumption, — to which it does not at all give these names, for they are to it things felt, — with faith, with a will of belief, with an emotional certainty, and finds its verification in an increasing spiritual intuition and experience. The philosophic mind accepts it calmly and discerningly for its coherent agreement with the facts and necessities of being; it verifies by a pervading and unfailing harmony with all the demands of reason and intellectualised intuition. But the sceptical mind — not the mind of mere doubt or dogmatic denial which usually arrogates that name, but the open and balanced mind of careful, impartial and reserved inquiry, — gives a certain provisional character to its hypotheses, and it verifies by the justification of whatever order or category of ascertainable facts it takes for its standard of proof and invests with a character of decisive authority or reality. There is room enough for all three methods and there is no reason why our complex modern mind should not proceed simultaneously by all of them at once. For if the sceptical or provisional attitude makes us more ready to modify our image of Truth in the light of new material of thought and knowledge, the religious mind also, provided it keeps a certain firm and profound openness to new spiritual experience, can proceed faster to a larger and larger light, and meanwhile we can walk by it with an assured step and go securely about our principal business of the growth and perfection of our being. The philosophic mind has the use of giving a needed largeness and openness to our mentality, — if it too does not narrow itself by a closed circle of metaphysical dogma, — and supports besides the harmony of our other action by the orderly assent of the higher reason.

In this matter of the soul and rebirth the initial hypothesis now lies quite open to us; the barrier has fallen. For if there is one thing now certain it is that physical science may give clues of process, but cannot lay hold on the reality of things. That means that the physical is not the whole secret of world and existence, and that in ourselves too the body is not the whole of our being. It is then through something supraphysical in Nature and ourselves which we may call the soul, whatever the exact substance of soul may be, that we are likely to get that greater truth and subtler experience which will enlarge the narrow rigid circle traced by physical science and bring us nearer to the Reality. There is nothing now to bar the most rational mind, — for true rationalism, real free thought need no longer be identified, as it was for some time too hastily and intolerantly, with a denial of the soul and a scouting of the truths of spiritual philosophy and religion, — there is nothing to prevent us from proceeding firmly upon whatever certitudes of spiritual experience have become to us the soil of our inner growth or the pillars on our road to self-knowledge. These are soul realities. But the exact frame we shall give to that knowledge, will best be built by farther spiritual experience aided by new enlarged intuitions, confirmed in the suggestions of a wide philosophic reason and fruitfully using whatever helpful facts we may get from the physical and the psychic sciences. These are truths of soul process; their full light must come by experimental knowledge and observation of the world without us and the world within.

The admission of the soul's existence does not of itself lead, by its own necessity, by any indispensable next step, to the acceptance of rebirth. It will only bring in this indispensable consequence if there is such a thing as a soul evolution which enforces itself always and is a constant part of the order of existence and the law of the time process. Moreover some kind of admission of an individual soul is a first condition of the truth of rebirth. For there is a plausible theory of existence which admits an All-Soul, a universal being and becoming of which the material world is some sensible result, but does not admit any at all abiding truth of our spiritual individuality. The All-Soul may continually develop, may slowly yet urgently evolve its becoming; but each individual man or apparent individual being is to this way of thinking only a moment of the All-Soul and its evolution; out of that it rises by the formation which we call birth and it sinks back into it by the dissolution which we call death. But this limiting idea can only stand if we credit a creative biological evolution and its instrument of physical heredity with the whole causation of all our mental and spiritual being; but in that case we have no real soul or spirit, our soul personality or spiritual becoming is a fruit of our life and body. Now the question of rebirth turns almost entirely upon the one fundamental question of the past of the individual being and its future. If the creation of the whole nature is to be credited to the physical birth, then the body, life and soul of the individual are only a continuation of the body, life and soul of his ancestry, and there is no room anywhere for soul rebirth. The individual man has no past being independent of them and can have no independent future; he can prolong himself in his progeny, — the child may be his second or continued self, as the Upanishad puts it, — but there is no other rebirth for him. No continued stream of individuality presided over by any mental or spiritual person victoriously survives the dissolution of the body. On the other hand, if there is any element in us, still more the most important of all, which cannot be so accounted for, but presupposes a past or admits a future evolution other than that of the race mind and the physical ancestry, then some kind of soul birth becomes a logical necessity.

Now it is just here that the claims of physical and vital evolution and heredity seem to fail, — as a cause of our whole mental and spiritual being. Certainly it has been shown that our body and the most physical part of our life action are very largely the results of heredity, but not in such a way as to exclude an assisting and perhaps really predominant psychical cause other than the ancestral contribution. It has been shown if you will that our conscious vitality and those parts of mind which depend upon it, something of temperament, something of character, certain impulses and predispositions, are to a great extent shaped — or is it only influenced? — by evolutionary heredity; but not that they are entirely due to this force, not that there is no soul, no spiritual entity which accepts and makes use of this instrumentation, but is not its created result or helplessly subject to it in its becoming. Still more are the higher parts of our mind marked with a certain stamp of spiritual independence. They are not altogether helpless formations of evolutionary heredity. But still all these things are evidently very much under the influence of environment and its pressures and opportunities. And we may draw from that, if we choose, a limiting conclusion; we may say that they are a phase of the universal soul, a part of the process of its evolution by selection; the race, not the individual, is the continuous factor and all our individual effort and acquisition, only in appearance, not really independent, ceases with death, except so much of our gain as is chosen to be carried on in the race by some secret will or conscious necessity in the universal being or the persistent becoming.

But when we come to our highest spiritual elements, we find that here we do arrive at a very clear and sovereign independence. We can carry on far beyond any determination by environment or the pressure of the race-soul our own soul evolution by the governing force of our spiritual nature. Quite apart from any evidence of an after life on other planes or any memory of past births, this is sufficient warrant for a refusal to accept as sufficient any theory of the ephemeral being of the individual and the sole truth of the evolutionary Universal. Certainly, the individual being is not thereby shown to be independent of the All-Soul; it may be nothing but a form of it in time. But it is sufficient for our purpose that it is a persistent soul form, not determined by the life of the body and ceasing with its dissolution, but persisting independently beyond. For if it is thus independent of the physical race continuity in the future, if it thus shows itself capable of determining its own future soul evolution in time, it must have had secretly such an independent existence all through and it must have been determining in reality, though no doubt by some other and indirect insistence, its past soul evolution too in time. Possibly it may exist in the All-soul only during the universal continuity, may have arisen from it in that, may pass into it eventually. Or on the contrary it may exist in it prior to, or it is better to say, independent of the universal continuity, and there may be some kind of eternal individual. But it is sufficient for the theory of rebirth that a secret soul continuity of the individual does exist and not alone a brute succession of bodies informed by the All-Soul with a quite ephemeral illusion of mental or spiritual individuality.

There are theories of existence which accept the individual soul, but not soul evolution. There is, for instance, that singular dogma of a soul without a past but with a future, created by the birth of the body but indestructible by the death of the body. But this is a violent and irrational assumption, an imagination unverified and without verisimilitude. It involves the difficulty of a creature beginning in time but enduring through all eternity, an immortal being dependent for its existence on an act of physical generation, yet itself always and entirely unphysical and independent of the body which results from the generation. These are objections insuperable to the reason. But there is too the difficulty that this soul inherits a past for which it is in no way responsible, or is burdened with mastering propensities imposed on it not by its own act, and is yet responsible for its future which is treated as if it were in no way determined by that often deplorable inheritance, *damnosa hereditas*, or that unfair creation, and were entirely of its own making. We are made helplessly what we are and are yet responsible for what we are,—or at least for what we shall be hereafter, which is inevitably determined to a large extent by what we are originally. And we have only this one chance. Plato and the Hottentot, the fortunate child of saints or Rishis and the born and trained criminal plunged from beginning to end in the lowest fetid corruption of a great modern city have equally to create by the action or belief of this one unequal life all their eternal future. This is a paradox which offends both the soul and the reason, the ethical sense and the spiritual intuition.

There is too the kindred idea, behind which a truth obscurely glimmers, that the soul of man is something high, pure and great which has fallen into the material existence and by its use of its nature and its acts in the body must redeem itself, must return to its own celestial nature. But it is evident that this one earthly life is not sufficient for all to effect that difficult return, but rather most may and do miss it entirely; and we have then either to suppose that an immortal soul can perish or be doomed to eternal perdition or else that it has more existences than this poor precarious one apparently given to it, lives or states of being which intervene between its fall and the final working out of a sure redemption. But the first supposition is subject to all the difficulties of that other paradox. Apart from the problem of the reason of the descent, it is difficult to see how straight from celestial being these different souls should have lapsed immediately to such immense differences of gradation in their fall and in such way that each is responsible for the otherwise cruel and unequal conditions under which he has to determine so summarily his eternal future. Each must surely have had a past which made him responsible for his present conditions, if he is to be held thus strictly to account for all their results and the use he makes of his often too scanty, grudging and sometimes quite hopeless opportunity. The very nature of our humanity supposes a varying constituent past for the soul as well as a resultant future.

More reasonable therefore is a recent theory which suggests that a spirit or mental being has descended from another and greater plane and taken up the material existence when the physical and the animal evolution had proceeded far enough for a human embodiment upon earth to be possible. He looks back to a long series of human lives, beginning from that point, which has brought each of us to his present condition, and forward to a still continuing series which will carry all by their own degrees and in their own time to whatever completion, transfiguration, return awaits the self-embodying human soul and is the crown of its long endeavour. But here again, what is it that brings about this connection of a spiritual being and higher mental nature and a physical being and lower animal nature? what necessitates this taking up of the lower life by the spirit which here becomes man? It would seem surely that there must have been some previous connection; the possessing mental or spiritual being must all the time have been preparing this lower life it thus occupies for a human manifestation. The whole evolution would then be an ordered continuity from the beginning and the intervention of mind and spirit would be no sudden inexplicable miracle, but a coming forward of that which was always there behind, an open taking up of the manifested life by a power which was always secretly presiding over the life evolution.

What this theory of rebirth supposes is an evolution of being in the material world from matter to embodied mind and a universal spirit which ensouls this evolution, while our individual spirits exist in the universal and follow their upward course to whatever purposed consummation or liberation or both may beckon to us at its end. Much more than this it may mean, but this at least; a soul evolution the real fact, an assumption of higher and higher forms the first appearance. We might indeed allow a past and future for the human soul, but place them below and above this terrestrial plane and admit only one casual or purposeful existence upon earth. But this would mean two orders of progressive existence unconnected and yet meeting for a brief moment. There would be an errant individual human soul intervening in the ordered terrestrial evolution and almost immediately passing out without any connecting cause or necessity. But especially it leaves insufficiently explained the phenomenon of the largely terrestrial animal being and nature of this spiritual and supra-terrestrial entity, this soul, its struggle for liberation, and the infinitely varying degrees in which in different bodies it has succeeded in dominating the lower nature. A past terrestrial soul evolution sufficiently accounting for these variations and degrees of our mixed being and a future soul evolution that helps us progressively to liberate the godhead of the spirit, seem the only just and reasonable explanation of this labour of a matter-shackled soul which has attained a variable degree of humanity in the midst of a general progressive appearance of the life, mind and spirit in a material universe. Rebirth is the only possible machinery for such a soul evolution.

The Significance of Rebirth

The one question which through all its complexities is the sum of philosophy and to which all human enquiry comes round in the end, is the problem of ourselves, — why we are here and what we are, and what is behind and before and around us, and what we are to do with ourselves, our inner significances and our outer environment. In the idea of evolutionary rebirth, if we can once find it to be a truth and recognise its antecedents and consequences, we have a very sufficient clue for an answer to all these connected sides of the one perpetual question. A spiritual evolution of which our universe is the scene and earth its ground and stage, though its plan is still kept back above from our yet limited knowledge, — this way of seeing existence is a luminous key which we can fit into many doors of obscurity. But we have to look at it in the right focus, to get its true proportions and, especially, to see it in its spiritual significance more than in its mechanical process. The failure to do that rightly will involve us in much philosophical finessing, drive on this side or the other to exaggerated negations and leave our statement of it, however perfect may be its logic, yet unsatisfying and unconvincing to the total intelligence and the complex soul of humanity.

The bare idea of repeated births as the process of our soul existence does not carry us much farther than the simple material reality of this single life in the body, that first fact of our conscious sensation and memory which is the occasion of all our speculations. Behind our present starting-point and preceding this one lappet of our race in the fields of being rebirth reminds us indeed of a past, of pregnant anterior courses, a soul-existence in many previous bodies which have immediately created what we now are. But to what use or advantage if there is no progressive significance in our preexistence and our persevering continuity? In front of us it rolls far back from our vision the obstruction of the near blank wall of death; our journeying upon earth becomes less of a long or brief unretraceable road ending abruptly and perplexingly in a cul-de-sac; our physical dissolution is robbed of the cruellest poison of its sting. For the burden of death to man the thinking, willing, feeling creature is not the loss of this poor case or chariot of body, but it is the blind psychical finality death suggests, the stupid material end of our will and thought and aspiration and endeavour, the brute breaking off of the heart's kind and sweet relations and affections, the futile convicting discontinuity of that marvellous and all-supporting soul-sense which gives us our radiant glimpses of the glory and delight of existence, — that is the discord and harsh inconsequence against which the thinking living creature revolts as incredible and inadmissible. The fiery straining to immortality of our life, mind, psyche, which can assent to cessation only by turning in enmity upon their own flame of nature, and the denial of it which the dull acquiescence of a body consenting inertly to death as to life brings in on us, is the whole painful irreconcilable contradiction of our double nature. Rebirth takes the difficulty and solves it in the sense of a soul continuity with a beat of physical repetition. Like other non-materialistic solutions it gives the right to the soul's suggestion as against the body's and sanctions the demand for survival, but unlike some others it justifies the bodily life by its utility to the soul's continued self-experience; our too swift act in the body ceases to be an isolated accident or an abrupt interlude, it gets the justification of a fulfilling future as well as a creating past for its otherwise haphazard actions and relations. But simple persistence, mechanical continuity is not enough; that is not all our psychical being signifies, not the whole luminous meaning of survival and continuity; without ascension, without expansion, without some growing up straight into light in the strength of our spirit our higher members toil here uncompleted, our birth in matter is not justified by any adequate meaning. We are very little better off than if death remained our ending; for our life in the end becomes then an indefinitely continued and renewed and temporarily consequent in place of an inconsequent, abruptly ended and soon convicted futility.

By rebirth, too, this world around us, our environment, its suggestions, its opportunities are no longer left as the field of an ephemeral physical flowering or as a Life which cares very little for and means very little to the individual, though it may offer much perhaps during its uncertain longer time to the species. The world grows to us a field of soul-experience, a system of soul recurrences, a means of self-effectuation, perhaps a crystallising of the conscious being's effective self-reflections. But to what end if our recurrence is only a repetition or a hesitating fluctuation within a few set types with a very limited, always uncompleted circle of accomplishment? For that is what it comes to, if there is no upward outlet, no infinite progression or no escape or enlarging into the soul's infinities. Rebirth tells us that what we are is a soul performing constantly the miracle of self-embodiment; but why this embodiment, what this soul has to do here with itself and what use it is to make of this world which is given to it for its grandiose scene, its difficult, plastic material and its besieging battery of multiform stimulus and suggestions, is hardly at all clearer than before. But the perception of rebirth as an occasion and means for a spiritual evolution fills in every hiatus. It makes life a significant ascension and not a mechanical recurrence; it opens to us the divine vistas of a growing soul; it makes the worlds a nexus of spiritual self-expansion; it sets us seeking, and with a sure promise to all of a great finding now or hereafter, for the self-knowledge of our spirit and the self-fulfilment of a wise and divine intention in our existence.

The oppressing sense of a circle of mechanical recurrence and the passionate seeking for an outlet of absolute escape haunted the earlier statements of the truth of rebirth and have left upon them in spite of the depths they fathomed a certain stamp of unsatisfactory inadequacy, — not illogical, for they are logical enough, once their premises are admitted, but unsatisfying, because they do not justify to us our being. For, missing the divine utility of the cosmic workings, they fail to explain to us with a sufficiently large, patient, steadfast wholeness God and ourselves and existence, negate too much, miss the positive sense of our strain and leave sounding an immense note of spiritual futility and cosmic discord. No statement of the sense of our being or our non-being has laid a more insistent stress on rebirth than did the Buddhistic; but it affirms strongly only the more strongly to negate. It views the recurrence of birth as a prolonged mechanical chain; it sees, with a sense of suffering and distaste, the eternal revolving of an immense cosmic wheel of energy with no divine sense in its revolutions, its beginning an affirmation of ignorant desire, its end a nullifying bliss of escape. The wheel turns uselessly for ever disturbing the peace of Non-being and creating souls whose one difficult chance and whole ideal business is to cease. That conception of being is only an extension from our first matter-governed sense of the universe, of our creation in it and of our decisive cessation. It takes up at every point our first obvious view of the bodily life and restates all its circumstances in the terms of a more psychical and spiritual idea of our existence.

What we see in the material universe is a stupendous system of mechanical recurrences. A huge mechanical recurrence rules that which is long-enduring and vast; a similar but frailer mechanical recurrence sways all that is ephemeral and small. The suns leap up into being, flame wheeling in space, squander force by motion and fade and are extinct, again perhaps to blaze into being and repeat their course, or else other suns take their place and fulfil their round. The seasons of Time repeat their unending and unchanging cycle. Always the tree of life puts forth its various flowers and sheds them and breaks into the same flowers in their recurring season. The body of man is born and grows and decays and perishes, but it gives birth to other bodies which maintain the one same futile cycle. What baffles the intelligence in all this intent and persistent process is that it seems to have in it no soul of meaning, no significance except the simple fact of causeless and purposeless existence dogged or relieved by the annulling or the compensating fact of individual cessation. And this is because we perceive the mechanism, but do not see the Power that uses the mechanism and the intention in its use. But the moment we know that there is a conscious Spirit self-wise and infinite brooding upon the universe and a secret slowly self-finding soul in things, we get to the necessity of an idea in its consciousness, a thing conceived, willed, set in motion and securely to be done, progressively to be fulfilled by these great deliberate workings.

But the Buddhistic statement admits no self, spirit or eternal Being in its rigorously mechanical economy of existence. It takes only the phenomenon of a constant becoming and elevates that from the physical to the psychical level. As there is evident to our physical mind an Energy, action, motion, capable of creating by its material forces the forms and powers of the material universe, so there is for the Buddhistic vision of things an Energy, action, Karma, creating by its psychic powers of idea and association this embodied soul life with its continuity of recurrences. As the body is a dissoluble construction, a composite and combination, so the soul too is a dissoluble construction and combination; the soul life like the physical life sustains itself by a continuous flux and repetition of the same workings and movements. As this constant hereditary succession of lives is a prolongation of the one universal principle of life by a continued creation of similar bodies, a mechanical recurrence, so the system of soul rebirth too is a constant prolongation of the principle of the soul-life by a continued creation through Karma of similar embodied associations and experiences, a mechanical recurrence. As the cause of all this physical birth and long hereditary continuation is an obscure will to life in Matter, so the cause of continued soul birth is an ignorant desire or will to be in the universal energy of Karma. As the constant wheelings of the universe and the motions of its forces generate individual existences who escape from or end in being by an individual dissolution, so there is this constant wheel of becoming and motion of Karma which forms into individualised soul-lives that must escape from their continuity by a dissolving cessation. An extinction of the embodied consciousness is our apparent material end; for soul too the end is extinction, the blank satisfaction of Nothingness or some ineffable bliss of a superconscient Non-Being. The affirmation of the mechanical occurrence or recurrence of birth is the essence of this view; but while the bodily life suffers an enforced end and dissolution, the soul life ceases by a willed self-extinction.

The Buddhistic theory adds nothing to the first obvious significance of life except an indefinite prolongation by rebirth which is a burden, not a gain, and the spiritual greatness of the discipline of self-extinction, — the latter, no doubt, a thing of great value. The illusionist solution adds something, but does not differ very greatly in its motive from the Buddhistic. It sets against the futile cosmic repetition an eternity of our own absolute being; from the ignorance which creates the illusory mechanism of a recurrence of rebirth, it escapes into the self-knowledge of our ineffable existence. That seems to bring in a positive strain and to give to our being an initial, a supporting and an eventual reality. But the hiatus here is the absence of all true and valid relation between this real being of ours and all our birth and becoming. The last event and end of our births is not represented as any absolute fulfilment of what we are, — that would be a great, fruitful and magnificently positive philosophy, nor as the final affirmation of a progressive self-finding, — that too would give a noble meaning to our existence; it is a turning away from the demand of the universal Spirit, a refusal of all these cosmic ideas, imaginations, aspirations, action and effectuation. The way to find our being given us is an absolute denial of all our becoming. We rise to self by a liberating negation of ourselves, and in the result the Idea in the universe pursues its monstrous and aimless road, but the individual ceases and is blest in the cessation. The motive of this way of thought is the same oppressive sense of an ignorant mechanical cosmic recurrence as in the Buddhistic and the same high impatient passion of escape. There is recognition of a divine source of life, but a non-recognition of any divine meaning in life. And as for rebirth it is reduced in its significance to a constant mechanism of self-deception, and the will not to live is shown us as the last acquisition, the highest good and the one desirable result of living. The satisfaction which Illusionism gives, — for it does give a certain high austere kind of satisfaction to the intellect and to one turn of spiritual tendency, — is the pressing to a last point of the obvious antinomy between this great burdensome and tyrannous mechanism, the universe, and the spirit which feels itself of another and a diviner nature, the great relief to a soul passioning for freedom, but compelled to labour on as a spring of the dull machine, of being able to cast away the cosmic burden, and finally the free and bare absoluteness of this spiritual conclusion. But it gives no real, because no fruitful answer to the problem of God and man and the significance of life; it only gets away from them by a skilful evasion and takes away from them all significance, so that any question of the sense and will in all this tremendous labour and throb and seeking loses meaning. But the challenge of God's universe to the knowledge and strength of the human spirit cannot in the end be met by man with a refusal or solved by an evasion, even though an individual soul may take refuge from the demand, as a man may from the burden of action and pain in unconsciousness, in spiritual trance or sleep or escape through its blank doors into the Absolute. Something the Spirit of the universe means by our labour in existence, some sense it has in these grandiose rhythms, and it has not undertaken them in an eternally enduring error or made them in a jest.[1] To know that and possess it, to find and fulfil consciously the universal being's hidden significances is the task given to the human spirit.

[1] The magnificent and pregnant phrase of the Koran, "Thinkest thou that I have made the heavens and the earth and all that is between them in a jest?"

There are other statements or colourings of the idea of rebirth which admit a more positive sense for existence and nourish a robuster confidence in the power and delight of being which are its secret fountains; but they all stumble in the end over the limitations of humanity and an inability to see any outlet from their bondage in the order of the universe, because they suppose this to be a thing fixed from of years sempiternal—*śāśvatībhyaḥ samābhyaḥ*, not an eternally developing and creative, but an immutable cycle. The Vaishnava idea of the play of God, striking as it does into the secret of the hidden delight at the core of things, is a luminous ray shot into the very heart of the mystery; but isolated it cannot solve all its enigma. There is more here in the world than a play of secret delight; there is knowledge, there is power, there is a will and a mighty labour. Rebirth so looked at becomes too much of a divine caprice with no object but its playing, and ours is too great and strenuous a world to be so accounted for. Such chequered delight as is given to our becoming, is a game of disguises and seekings with no promise here of any divine completeness; its circles seem in the end not worth following out and the soul turns gladly to its release from the game's unsatisfying mazes. The Tantric solution shows us a supreme superconscient Energy which casts itself out here into teeming worlds and multitudinous beings and in its order the soul rises from birth to birth and follows its million forms, till in a last human series it opens to the consciousness and powers of its own divinity and returns through them by a rapid illumination to the eternal superconscience. We find at last the commencement of a satisfying synthesis, some justification of existence, a meaningful consequence in rebirth, a use and a sufficient though only temporary significance for the great motion of the cosmos. On lines very like these the modern mind, when it is disposed to accept rebirth, is inclined to view it. But there is a too minor stress on the soul's divine potentialities, a haste of insistence on the escape into superconscience; the supreme Energy constructs too long and stupendous a preparation for so brief and so insufficient a flowering. There is a lacuna here, some secret is still missing.

There are certain limitations of our own thought over which all these solutions stumble, and the chief of these obstacles are our sense of the mechanical nature of the universe and our inability to see forward to a greater than our present type of humanity. We see the superconscient Spirit in its effulgence and freedom and we see the universe in its inconscient bondage to the cycle of its mechanical recurrences, or we see existence as an abstract entity and Nature as a mechanical force; the conscient soul stands between as a link between these opposites, but it is itself so incomplete that we cannot find in this link the secret or make of it a strong master of reconciliation. Then we pronounce birth to be an error of the soul and see our one chance of liberation in a shaking off of these natal shackles and a violent reversion to supracosmic consciousness or the freedom of abstract being. But what if rebirth were in truth no long dragging chain, but rather at first a ladder of the soul's ascension and at last a succession of mighty spiritual opportunities? It will be so if the infinite existence is not what it seems to the logical intellect, an abstract entity, but what it is to intuition and in deeper soul experience, a conscious spiritual Reality, and that Reality as real here as in any far off absolute Superconscience. For then universal Nature would be no longer a mechanism with no secret but its own inconscient mechanics and no intention but the mere recurrent working; it would be the conscient energy of the universal Spirit hidden in the greatness of its processes, *mahimānam asya*. And the soul ascending from the sleep of matter through plant and animal life to the human degree of the power of life and there battling with ignorance and limit to take possession of its royal and infinite kingdom would be the mediator appointed to unfold in Nature the spirit who is hidden in her subtleties and her vastnesses. That is the significance of life and the world which the idea of evolutionary rebirth opens to us; life becomes at once a progressive ascending series for the unfolding of the Spirit. It acquires a supreme significance: the way of the Spirit in its power is justified, no longer a foolish and empty dream, an eternal delirium, great mechanical toil or termless futility, but the sum of works of a large spiritual Will and Wisdom: the human soul and the cosmic spirit look into each other's eyes with a noble and divine meaning.

The questions which surround our existence elucidate themselves at once with a certain satisfactory fullness. What we are is a soul of the transcendent Spirit and Self unfolding itself in the cosmos in a constant evolutionary embodiment of which the physical side is only a pedestal of form corresponding in its evolution to the ascending degrees of the spirit, but the spiritual growth is the real sense and motive. What is behind us is the past terms of the spiritual evolution, the upward gradations of the spirit already climbed, by which through constant rebirth we have developed what we are, and are still developing this present and middle human term of the ascension. What is around us is the constant process of the unfolding in its universal aspect: the past terms are there contained in it, fulfilled, overpassed by us, but in general and various type still repeated as a support and background; the present terms are there not as an unprofitable recurrence, but in active pregnant gestation of all that is yet to be unfolded by the spirit, no irrational decimal recurrence helplessly repeating for ever its figures, but an expanding series of powers of the Infinite. What is in front of us is the greater potentialities, the steps yet unclimbed, the intended mightier manifestations. Why we are here is to be this means of the spirit's upward self-unfolding. What we have to do with ourselves and our signifi-cances is to grow and open them to greater significances of divine being, divine consciousness, divine power, divine delight and multiplied unity, and what we have to do with our environment is to use it consciously for increasing spiritual purposes and make it more and more a mould for the ideal unfolding of the perfect nature and self-conception of the Divine in the cosmos. This is surely the Will in things which moves, great and deliberate, unhasting, unresting, through whatever cycles, towards a greater and greater informing of its own finite figures with its own infinite Reality.

All this is to the mind that lives in the figures of the present, as it must be to the careful sceptical mind of positive inquiry, no more than a hypothesis; for if evolution is an acknowledged idea, rebirth itself is only a supposition. Take it so, but still it is a better hypothesis than the naive and childlike religious solutions which make the world an arbitrary caprice and man the breathing clay puppet of an almighty human-minded Creator, and at least as good a hypothesis as the idea of a material inconscient Force somehow stumbling into a precarious, ephemeral, yet always continued phenomenon of consciousness, or a creative Life la-bouring in the Bergsonian formula oppressed but constant in the midst of a universal death, as good too as the idea of a mechanical working of Prakriti, Maya, Shakti into which or in which a real or unreal individual stumbles and wanders, *dandramyamāṇaḥ an-*

dhena nīyamāno yathāndhaḥ,[1] until he can get out of it by a spiritual liberation. To a large philosophical questioning it will not seem in disagreement with the known lines of existence or out of tune with the facts and necessities of being or the demands of reason and intuition, even though it admits a yet unrealised factor, things yet to be; for that is implied in the very idea of evolution. It may modify, but does not radically contradict any religious experience or aspiration,— for it is not inconsistent either with a union with Superconscience or bliss in heavens beyond or any personal or impersonal relation with the Divine, since these may well be heights of the spiritual unfolding. Its truth will depend on spiritual experience and effectuation; but chiefly on this momentous issue, whether there is anything in the soul-powers of man which promises a greater term of being than his present mentality and whether that greater term can be made effective for his embodied existence? That is the question which remains over to be tested by psychological inquiry and the problem to be resolved in the course of the spiritual evolution of man.

There are transcendental questions of the metaphysical necessity, possibility, final reality of an evolutionary manifestation of this kind, but they do not need to be brought in now and here; for the time we are concerned only with its reality to experience and with the processional significance of rebirth, with the patent fact that we are a part of some kind of manifestation and move forward in the press of some kind of evolution. We see a Power at work and seek whether in that power there is a conscious Will, an ordered development and have first to discover whether it is the blind result of an organised Chance or inconscient self-compelled Law or the plan of a universal Intelligence or Wisdom. Once we find that there is a conscious Spirit of which this movement is one expression, or even admit that as our working hypothesis, we are bound to go on and ask whether this developing order ceases with what man now is or is laden with something more towards which it and he have to grow, an unfinished expression, a greater unfound term, and in that case it is evidently towards that greater thing that man must be growing; to prepare it and to realise it must be the stage beyond in his destiny. Towards that new step in the evolution his history as a race must be subconsciently tending and the powers of the highest individuals half consciously striving to be delivered

[1] "Beating about like the blind led by the blind."

of this greater birth; and since the ascending order of rebirth follows always the degrees of the evolution, that too cannot be meant to stop short or shoot off abruptly into the superconscient without any regard to the intended step. The relation of our birth to life on other levels of consciousness and to whatever transcendent Superconscience there may be, are important problems, but their solution must be something in harmony with the intention of the Spirit in the universe; all must be part of a unity, and not an imbroglio of spiritual incoherences and contradictions. Our first bridge from the known to the unknown on this line of thought must be to discover how far the yet unfinished ladder of evolution can mount in the earth series. The whole processional significance of rebirth may be wrapped up in that one yet unattempted discovery.

The Ascending Unity

The human mind loves a clear simplicity of view; the more trenchant a statement, the more violently it is caught by it and inclined to acceptance. This is not only natural to our first crudity of thinking, and the more attractive because it makes things delightfully easy to handle and saves an immense amount of worry of enquiry and labour of reflection, but, modified, it accompanies us to the higher levels of a more watchful mentality. Alexander's method with the fateful knot is our natural and favourite dealing with the tangled web of things, the easy cut, the royal way, the facile philosophy of this and not this, that and not that, a strong yes and no, a simple division, a pair of robust opposites, a clean cut of classification. Our reason acts by divisions, even our ordinary illogical thought is a stumbling and bungling summary analysis and arrangement of the experience that offers itself to us with such unending complexity. But the cleanest and clearest division is that which sets us most at ease, because it impresses on our still childlike intelligence a sense of conclusive and luminous simplicity.

But the average mind enamoured of a straight and plain thinking, for which, for a famous instance, that great doctor Johnson thought with the royal force dear to all strong men when he destroyed Berkeley's whole philosophy by simply kicking a stone and saying "There I prove the reality of matter," is not alone affected by this turn towards simple solutions. Even the philosopher, though he inclines to an intricate reasoning by the way, is best delighted when he can get by it to some magnificently conclusive conclusion, some clean-cutting distinction between Brahman and non-Brahman, Reality and unreality or any of the host of mental oppositions on which so many "isms" have been founded. These royal roads of philosophy have the advantage that they are highly and grandly cut for the steps of the metaphysical intellect and at the same time attract and overpower the ordinary mind by the grandiose eminence of the peak in which they end, some snow-white heaven-cutting Matterhorn of sovereign formula. What a magnificent exterminating sweep do we hear for instance in that old renowned sentence, *brahma satyaṁ jagan mithyā*, the Eternal alone is true, the universe is a lie, and how these four victorious words seem to settle the whole business of God and man and world and life at once and for ever in their uncompromising antithesis of affirmation and negation. But after all perhaps when we come to think more at large about the matter, we may find that Nature and Existence are not of the same mind as man in this respect, that there is here a great complexity which we must follow with patience and that those ways of thinking have most chance of a fruitful truth-yielding, which like the inspired thinking of the Upanishads take in many sides at once and reconcile many conflicting conclusions. One can hew material for a hundred philosophies out of the Upanishads as if from some bottomless Titan's quarry and yet no more exhaust it than one can exhaust the opulent bosom of our mother Earth or the riches of our father Ether.

Man began this familiar process of simple cuttings by emphasizing his sense of himself as man; he made of himself a being separate, unique and peculiar in this world, for whom or round whom everything else was supposed to be created, — and all the rest, the subhuman existence, animal, plant, inanimate object, everything to the original atom seemed to him a creation different from himself, separate, of another nature; he condemned all to be without a soul, he was the one ensouled being. He saw life, defined it by certain characters that struck his mind, and set apart all other existence as non-living, inanimate. He looked at his earth, made it the centre of the universe, because the one inhabited scene of embodied souls or living beings; but the innumerable other heavenly bodies were only lights to illumine earth's day or to relieve her night. He perceived the insufficiency of this one earthly life only to create another opposite definition of a perfect heavenly existence and set it in the skies he saw above him. He perceived his "I" or self and conceived of it as a separate embodied ego, the centre of all his earthly and heavenly interests, and cut off all other being as the not-I which was there for him to make the best use he could out of it for this little absorbing entity. When he looked beyond these natural sense-governed divisions, he still followed the same logical policy. Conceiving of spirit, he cut it off sharply as a thing by itself, the opposite of all that was not spirit; an antinomy between spirit and matter became the base of his self-conception, or else more amply between spirit on the one side and on the other mind, life and body. Then conceiving of self as a pure entity, all else being not-self was separated from it as of quite another character. Incidentally, with the eye of his inveterate dividing mind, he saw it as his own separate self and, just as before he had made the satisfaction of ego his whole business on earth, so he made the soul's own individual salvation its one all-important spiritual and heavenly transaction. Or he saw the universal and denied the reality of the individual, refusing to them any living unity or co-existent reality, or saw a transcendent Absolute separate from individual and universe so that these became a figment of the unreal, Asat. Being and Becoming are to his clean-cutting confidently trenchant mind two opposite categories, of which one or the other must be denied, or made a temporary construction or a sum, or sicklied over with the pale hue of illusion, and not Becoming accepted as an eternal display of Being. These conceptions of the sense-guided or the intellectual reason still pursue us, but a considering wisdom comes more and more to perceive that conclusive and satisfying as they may seem and helpful though they may be for action of life, action of mind, action of spirit, they are yet, as we now put them, constructions. There is a truth behind them, but a truth which does not really permit of these isolations. Our classifications set up too rigid walls; all borders are borders only and not impassable gulfs. The one infinitely variable Spirit in things carries over all of himself into each form of his omnipresence; the self, the Being is at once unique in each, common in our collectivities and one in all beings. God moves in many ways at once in his own indivisible unity.

The conception of man as a separate and quite peculiar being in the universe has been rudely shaken down by a patient and disinterested examination of the process of nature. He is without equal or peer and occupies a privileged position on earth, but is not solitary in his being; all the evolution is there to explain this seeker of spiritual greatness embodied in a fragile body and narrow life and bounded mind who in turn by his being and seeking explains to itself the evolution. The animal prepares and imperfectly prefigures man and is itself prepared in the plant, as that too is foreseen obscurely by all that precedes it in the terrestrial expansion. Man himself takes up the miraculous play of the electron and atom, draws up through the complex development of the protoplasm the chemical life of subvital things, perfects the original nervous system of the plant in the physiology of the completed animal being, consummates and repeats rapidly in his embryonic growth the past evolution of the animal form into the human perfection and, once born, rears himself from the earthward and downward animal proneness to the erect figure of the spirit who is already looking up to his farther heavenward evolution. All the terrestrial past of the world is there summarised in man, and not only has Nature given as it were the physical sign that she has formed in him an epitome of her universal forces, but psychologically also he is one in his subconscient being with her obscurer subanimal life, contains in his mind and nature the animal and rises out of all this substratum into his conscious manhood.

Whatever soul there is in man is not a separate spiritual being which has no connection with all the rest of the terrestrial family, but seems to have grown out of it by a taking up of it all and an exceeding of its sense by a new power and meaning of the spirit. This is the universal nature of the type man on earth, and it is reasonable to suppose that whatever has been the past history of the individual soul, it must have followed the course of the universal nature and evolution. The separative pride which would break up the unity of Nature in order to make of ourselves another as well as a greater creation, has no physical warrant, but has been found on the contrary to be contradicted by all the evidence; and there is no reason to suppose that it has any spiritual justification. The physical history of humankind is the growth out of the subvital and the animal life into the greater power of manhood; our inner history as indicated by our present nature, which is the animal plus something that exceeds it, must have been a simultaneous and companion growing on the same curve into the soul of humanity. The ancient Indian idea which refused to separate nature of man from the universal Nature or self of man from the one common self, accepted this consequence of its seeing. Thus the Tantra assigns eighty millions of plant and animal lives as the sum of the preparation for a human birth and, without binding ourselves to the figure, we can appreciate the force of its idea of the difficult soul evolution by which humanity has come or perhaps constantly comes into being. We can only get away from this necessity of an animal past by denying all soul to subhuman nature.

But this denial is only one of the blind, hasty and presump-

tuous isolations of the human mind which shut up in its own prison
of separate self-perception refuses to see its kinship with the rest of
natural being. Because soul or spirit works in the animal on a
lower scale, we are not warranted in thinking that there is no soul
in him, any more than a divine or superhuman being would be
justified in regarding us as soulless bodies or soulless minds
because of the grovelling downward drawn inferiority of our half-
animal nature. The figure which we use when sometimes we say of
one of our own kind that he has no soul, is only a figure; it means
only that the animal type of soul predominates in him over the
more developed soul type which we expect in the finer spiritual
figure of humanity. But this animal element is present in every
mother's son of us; it is our legacy, our inheritance from the
common earth-mother: and how spiritually do we get this element
of our being or incur the burden of this inheritance, if it is not the
earning of our own past, the power we have kept from a bygone
formative experience? The spiritual law of Karma is that the
nature of each being can be only the result of his past energies; to
suppose a soul which assumes and continues a past karma that is
not its own, is to cut a line of dissociation across this law and bring
in an unknown and unverified factor. But if we admit it, we must
account for that factor, we must explain or discover by what law,
by what connection, by what necessity, by what strange impulsion
of choice a spirit pure of all animal nature assumes a body and
nature of animality prepared for it by a lower order of being. If
there is no affinity and no consequence of past identity or
connection, this becomes an unnatural and impossible assumption.
Then it is the most reasonable and concordant conclusion that man
has the animal nature, — and indeed if we consider well his
psychology, we find that he houses many kinds of animal souls or
rather an amalgam of animal natures, — because the developing
self in him like the developed body has had a past subhuman
evolution. This conclusion preserves the unity of Nature and its
developing order; and it concurs with the persistent evidence of an
interaction and parallelism which we perceive between the inward
and the outward, the physical and the mental phenomenon, — a
correspondence and companionship which some would explain by
making mind a result and notation of the act of nerve and body,
but which can now be better accounted for by seeing in vital and
physical phenomenon a consequence and minor notation of a soul-

action which it at the same time hints and conceals from our sense-bound mentality. Finally, it makes of soul or spirit, no longer a miraculous accident or intervention in a material universe, but a constant presence in it and the secret of its order and its existence.

The concession of an animal soul existence and of its past subhuman births slowly and guardedly preparing the birth into humanity cannot stop short at this abrupt line in the natural gradation. For man epitomises in his being not only the animal existence below him, but the obscurer subanimal being. But if it is difficult for us to concede a soul to the despised animal form and mind, it is still more difficult to concede it to the brute sub-conscience of the subanimal nature. Ancient belief made this concession with the happiest ease, saw a soul, a living godhead everywhere in the animate and in the inanimate and nothing was to its view void of a spiritual existence. The logical abstracting intellect with its passion for clean sections intermediately swept away these large beliefs as an imaginative superstition or a primitive animism and, mastered by its limiting and dividing definitions, it drove a trenchant sectional cleavage between man and animal, animal and plant, animate and inanimate being. But now to the eye of our enlarging reason this system of intolerant cleavages is in rapid course of disappearance. The human mind is a development from what is inchoate in the animal mentality; there is, even, in that inferior type a sort of suppressed reason, for that name may well be given to a power of instinctive and customary conclusion from experience, association, memory and nervous response, and man himself begins with these things though he develops out of this animal inheritance a free human self-detaching power of reflective will and intelligence. And it is now clear that the nervous life which is the basis of that physical mentality in man and animal, exists also in the plant with a fundamental identity; not only so, but it is akin to us by a sort of nervous psychology which amounts to the existence of a sup-pressed mind. A subconscient mind in the plant, it is now not unreasonable to suggest, — but is it not at the summits of plant experience only half subconscious? — becomes conscient in the animal body. When we go lower down, we find hints that there are involved in the subvital most brute material forms the rudiments of precisely the same energy of life and its responses.

And the question then arises whether there is not an un-

broken continuity in Nature, no scissions and sections, no unbridgeable gulfs or impassable borders, but a complete unity,
matter instinct with a suppressed life, life instinct with a suppressed mind, mind instinct with a suppressed energy of a diviner
intelligence, each new form or type of birth evolving a stage in the
succession of suppressed powers, and there too the evolution not
at an end, but this large and packed intelligence the means of
liberating a greater and now suppressed self-power of the Spirit. A
spiritual evolution thus meets our eye in the world which an inner
force raises up a certain scale of gradations of its births in form by
the unfolding of its own hidden powers to the greatness of its
complete and highest reality. The word of the ancient Veda
stands, — out of all the ocean of inconscience, *apraketaṁ salilaṁ
sarvam idam*, it is that one spiritual Existent who is born by the
greatness of his own energy, *tapasas tan mahinā ajāyata ekam*.
Where in this evolution does the thing we call soul make its first
appearance? One is obliged to ask, was it not there, must it not
have been there from the first beginnings, even though asleep or,
as we may say, somnambulist in matter? If man were only a
superior animal with a greater range of physical mind, we might
conceivably say that there was no soul or spirit, but only three
successive powers of Energy in a series of the forms of matter. But
in this human intelligence there does appear at its summit a greater
power of spirit; we rise up to a consciousness which is not limited
by its physical means and formulas. This highest thing is not, as it
might first appear, an unsubstantial sublimation of mind and mind
a subtle sublimation of living matter. This greatness turns out to
have been the very self-existent substance and power of our being;
all other things seem in comparison only its lesser forms of itself
which it uses for a progressive revelation; spirit in the end proves
itself the first and not only the last, Alpha as well as Omega, and
the whole secret of existence from its beginning. We come to a
fathomless conception of this all, *sarvam idam*, in which we see
that there is an obscure omnipresent life in matter, activised by
that life a secret sleeping mind, sheltered in that sleep of mind an
involved all-knowing all-originating Spirit. But then soul is not to
be conceived of as a growth or birth of which we can fix a date of
its coming or a stage in the evolution which brings it to a first
capacity of formation, but rather all here is assumption of form by
a secret soul which becomes in the self-seeking of life increasingly

manifest to a growing self-conscience. All assumption of form is a constant and yet progressive birth or becoming of the soul, *sambhava*, *sambhūti*, — the dumb and blind and brute is that and not only the finely, mentally conscious human or the animal existence. All this infinite becoming is a birth of the Spirit into form. This is the truth, obscure at first or vague to the intelligence, but very luminous to an inner experience, on which the ancient Indian idea of rebirth took its station.

But the repeated birth of the same individual does not at first sight seem to be indispensable in this overpowering universal unity. To the logical intellect it might appear to be a contradiction, since all here is the one self, spirit, existence born into nature, assuming a multitude of forms, ascending many gradations of its stages of self-revelation. That summary cutting of existence into the I and the not-I which was the convenience of our egoistic notion of things, a turn of mind so powerful for action, would seem to be only a practical or a mechanical device of the one Spirit to support its separative phenomenon of birth and conscious variation of combined proceeding, a sorcerer's trick of the universal intelligence; it is only apparent fact of being, not its truth, — there is no separation, only a universal unity, one spirit. But may not this again be a swinging away to the opposite extreme? As the ego was an excessive scission in the unity of being, so this idea of an ocean of unity in which our life would be only an inconstant momentary wave, may be a violent excision of something indispensable to the universal order. Individuality is as important a thing to the ways of the Spirit of existence as universality. The individual is that potent secret of its being upon which the universal stresses and leans and makes the knot of power of all its workings: as the individual grows in consciousness and sight and knowledge and all divine power and quality, increasingly he becomes aware of the universal in himself, but aware of himself too in the universality, of his own past not begun and ended in the single transient body, but opening to future consummations. If the aim of the universal in our birth is to become self-conscient and possess and enjoy its being, still it is done through the individual's flowering and perfection; if to escape from its own workings be the last end, still it is the individual that escapes while the universal seems content to continue its multitudinous births to all eternity. Therefore the individual would appear to be a real power of the

Spirit and not a simple illusion or device, except in so far as the universal too may be, as some would have it, an immense illusion or a grand imposed device. On this line of thinking we arrive at the idea of some great spiritual existence of which universal and individual are two companion powers, pole and pole of its manifestation, indefinite circumference and multiple centre of the activised realities of its being.

This is a way of seeing things, harmonious at least in its complexity, supple and capable of a certain all-embracing scope, which we can take as a basis for our ideas of rebirth, — an ascending unity, a spirit involved in material existence which scales wonderfully up many gradations through life to organised mind and beyond mind to the evolution of its own complete self-conscience, the individual following that gradation and the power for its self-crowning. If human mind is the last word of its possibility on earth, then rebirth must end in man and proceed by some abrupt ceasing either to an existence on other planes or to an annulment of its spiritual circle. But if there are higher powers of the spirit which are attainable by birth, then the ascent is not finished, greater assumptions may lie before the soul which has now reached and is lifted to a perfecting of the high scale of humanity. It may even be that this ascending rebirth is not the long upward rocket shooting of a conscious being out of matter or its whirling motion in mind destined to break up and dissolve in some high air of calm nothingness or of silent timeless infinity, but a progress to some great act and high display of the Divinity which shall give a wise and glorious significance to his persistent intention in an eternal creation. Or that at least may be one power of the Eternal's infinite potentiality.

Involution and Evolution

The western idea of evolution is the statement of a process of formation, not an explanation of our being. Limited to the physical and biological data of Nature, it does not attempt except in a summary or a superficial fashion to discover its own meaning, but is content to announce itself as the general law of a quite mysterious and inexplicable energy. Evolution becomes a problem in motion which is satisfied to work up with an automatic regularity its own puzzle, but not to work it out, because, since it is only a process, it has no understanding of itself, and, since it is a blind perpetual automatism of mechanical energy, it has neither an origin nor an issue. It began perhaps or is always beginning; it will stop perhaps in time or is always somewhere stopping and going back to its beginnings, but there is no why, only a great turmoil and fuss of a how to its beginning and its cessation; for there is in its acts no fountain of spiritual intention, but only the force of an unresting material necessity. The ancient idea of evolution was the fruit of a philosophical intuition, the modern is an effort of scientific observation. Each as enounced misses something, but the ancient got at the spirit of the movement where the modern is content with a form and the most external machinery. The Sankhya thinker gave us the psychological elements of the total evolutionary process, analysed mind and sense and the subtle basis of matter and divined some of the secrets of the executive energy, but had no eye for the detail of the physical labour of Nature. He saw in it too not only the covering active evident Force, but the concealed sustaining spiritual entity, though by an excess of the analytic intellect, obsessed with its love of trenchant scissions and symmetrical oppositions, he set between meeting Soul and Force an original and eternal gulf or line of separation. The modern scientist strives to make a complete scheme and institution of the physical method which he has detected in its minute workings, but is blind to the miracle each step involves or content to lose the sense of it in the satisfied observation of a vast ordered phenomenon. But always the marvel of the thing remains, one with the inexplicable wonder of all existence, — even as it is said in the ancient Scripture,

> *āścaryavat paśyati kaścid enam*
> *āścaryavad vadati tathaiva cānyaḥ;*
> *āścaryavac cainam anyaḥ śṛṇoti,*
> *śrutvāpyenaṁ veda na caiva kaścit.*

"One looks on it and sees a miracle, another speaks of it as a miracle, as a miracle another hears of it, but what it is, for all the hearing, none knoweth." We know that an evolution there is, but not what evolution is; that remains still one of the initial mysteries of Nature.

For evolution, as is the habit with the human reason's accounts and solutions of the deep and unfathomable way of the spirit in things, raises more questions than it solves; it does not do away with the problem of creation, for all its appearance of solid orderly fact, any more than the religious affirmation of an external omnipotent Creator could do it or the illusionist's mystic Maya, *aghaṭana-ghaṭana-paṭīyasī*, very skilful in bringing about the impossible, some strange existent non-existent Power with an idea in That which is beyond and without ideas, self-empowered to create an existent non-existent world, existent because it very evidently is, non-existent because it is a patched up consistency of dreamful unreal transiences. The problem is only prolonged, put farther back, given a subtle and orderly, but all the more challengingly complex appearance. But, even when our questioning is confined to the one issue of evolution alone, the difficulty still arises of the essential significance of the bare outward facts observed, what is meant by evolution, what is it that evolves, from what and by what force of necessity? The scientist is content to affirm an original matter or substance, atomic, electric, etheric or whatever it may finally turn out to be, which by the very nature of its own inherent energy or of an energy acting in it and on it,—the two things are not the same, and the distinction, though it may seem immaterial in the beginning of the process, is of a considerable ultimate consequence,—produces owing to some unexplained law, constant system of results or other unalterable principle a number of different basic forms and powers of matter or different sensible and effective movements of energy: these come into being, it seems, when the minute original particles of matter meet together in variously disposed quantities, measures and combinations, and all the rest is a varying, developing, mounting movement of organised energy and its evolutionary consequences, *pariṇāma*, which depends on this crude constituting basis. All that is or may be a correct statement of phenomenal fact,—but we must not forget that the fundamental theory of science has been going of late through a considerable commotion of an upsetting and a rapid rearrangement,—but it carries us no step farther towards the principal, the all-important thing that we want to know. The way in which man sees and experiences the universe, imposes on his reason the necessity of a one original eternal substance of which all things are the forms and a one eternal original energy of which all movement of action and consequence is the variation. But the whole question is what is the reality of this substance and what is the essential nature of this energy?

Then, even if we suppose the least explicable part of the action to be an evolutionary development of the immaterial from Matter, still is that development a creation or a liberation, a birth of what did not exist before or a slow bringing out of what already existed in suppressed fact or in eternal potentiality? And the interest of the question becomes acute, its importance incalculable when we come to the still unexplained phenomenon of life and mind. Is life a creation out of inanimate substance or the appearance of a new, a suddenly or slowly resultant power out of the brute material energy, and is conscious mind a creation out of inconscient or subconscient life, or do these powers and godheads appear because they were always there though in a shrouded and by us unrecognizable condition of their hidden or suppressed idea and activity, Nomen and Numen? And what of the soul and of man? Is soul a new result or creation of our mentalised life, —even so many regard it, because it clearly appears as a self-conscious, bright, distinguishable power only when thinking life has reached some high pitch of its intensity,—or is it not a permanent entity, the original mystery that now unveils its hidden form, the eternal companion of the energy we call Nature, her secret inhabitant or her very spirit and reality? And is man a biological creation of a brute energy which has somehow unexpectedly and quite inexplicably managed to begin to feel and think, or is he in his real self that inner Being and Power which is the whole sense of the evolution and the master of Nature? Is Nature only the force of self-expression, self-formation, self-creation of a secret spirit, and man however hedged in his present capacity, the first being in Nature in whom that power begins to be consciently self-creative in the front of the action, in this outer chamber of physical being, there set to work and bring out by an increasingly self-conscious evolution what he can of all its human significance or its divine possibility? That is the clear conclusion we must arrive at in the end, if we once admit as the key of the whole movement, the reality of this whole mounting creation a spiritual evolution.

The word evolution carries with it in its intrinsic sense, in the idea at its root the necessity of a previous involution. We must, if a hidden spiritual being is the secret of all the action of Nature, give its full power to that latent value of the idea. We are bound then to suppose that all that evolves already existed involved, passive or otherwise active, but in either case concealed from us in the shell of material Nature. The Spirit which manifests itself here in a body, must be involved from the beginning in the whole of matter and in every knot, formation and particle of matter; life, mind and whatever is above mind must be latent inactive or concealed active powers in all the operations of material energy. The only alternative would be to drive in between the two sides of our being the acute Sankhya scission; but that divides too much spirit and nature. Nature would be an inert and mechanical thing, but she would set to her work activised by some pressure on her of the Spirit. Spirit would be Being conscious and free in its own essence from the natural activity, but would phenomenally modify or appear to modify its consciousness in response to some reaction of Nature. One would reflect the movements of the active Power, the other would enlighten her activities with the consciousness of the self-aware immortal being. In that case the scientific evolutionary view of Nature as a vast mechanical energy, life, mind and natural soul action its scale of developing operations would have a justification. Our consciousness would only be a luminous translation of the self-driven unresting mechanical activity into responsive notes of experience of the consenting spiritual witness. But the disabling difficulty in this notion is the quite opposite character of our own highest seeing; for in the end and as the energy of the universal force mounts up the gradients of its own possibilities, Nature becomes always more evidently a power of the spirit and all her mechanism only figures of its devising mastery. The power of the Flame cannot be divided from the

Flame; where the Flame is, there is the power, and where the power is there is the fiery Principle. We have to come back to the idea of a spirit present in the universe and, if the process of its works of power and its appearance is in the steps of an evolution, there imposes itself the necessity of a previous involution.

This spirit in things is not apparent from the beginning, but self-betrayed in an increasing light of manifestation. We see the compressed powers of Nature start released from their original involution, disclose in a passion of work the secrets of their infinite capacity, press upon themselves and on the supporting inferior principle to subject its lower movement on which they are forced to depend into a higher working proper to their own type and feel their proper greatness in the greatness of their self-revealing effectuations. Life takes hold of matter and breathes into it the numberless figures of its abundant creative force, its subtle and variable patterns, its enthusiasm of birth and death and growth and act and response, its will of more and more complex organ-isation of experience, its quivering search and feeling out after a self-consciousness of its own pleasure and pain and understanding gust of action; mind seizes on life to make it an instrument for the wonders of will and intelligence; soul possesses and lifts mind through the attraction of beauty and good and wisdom and greatness towards the joy of some half-seen ideal highest exist-ence; and in all this miraculous movement and these climbing greatnesses each step sets its foot on a higher rung and opens to a clearer, larger and fuller scope and view of the always secret and always self-manifesting spirit in things. The eye fixed on the physical evolution has only the sight of a mechanical grandeur and subtlety of creation; the evolution of life opening to mind, the evolution of mind opening to the soul of its own light and action, the evolution of soul out of the limited powers of mind to a resplendent blaze of the infinities of spiritual being are the more significant things, give us greater and subtler reaches of the self-disclosing Secrecy. The physical evolution is only an outward sign, the more and more complex and subtle development of a sup-porting structure, the growing exterior metre mould of form which is devised to sustain in matter the rising intonations of the spiritual harmony. The spiritual significance finds us as the notes rise; but not till we get to the summit of the scale can we command the integral meaning of that for which all these first formal measures were made the outward lines, the sketch or the crude notation. Life itself is only a coloured vehicle, physical birth a convenience for the greater and greater births of the Spirit.

The spiritual process of evolution is then in some sense a creation, but a self-creation, not a making of what never was, but a bringing out of what was implicit in the Being. The Sanskrit word for creation signifies a loosing forth, a letting out into the workings of Nature. The Upanishad in a telling figure applies the image of the spider which brings its web out of itself and creates the structure in which it takes its station. That is applied in the ancient Scripture not to the evolution of things out of Matter, but to an original bringing of temporal becoming out of the eternal infinity; Matter itself and this material universe are only such a web or indeed no more than a part of it brought out from the spiritual being of the Infinite. But the same truth, the same law holds good of all that we see of the emergence of things from involution in the material energy. We might almost speak here of a double evolution. A Force inherent in the Infinite brings out of it eternally the structure of its action in a universe of which the last descending scale is based upon an involution of all the powers of the spirit into an inconscient absorption in her self-oblivious passion of form and structural working. Thence comes an ascent and progressive liberation of power after power till the spirit self-disclosed and set free by knowledge and mastery of its works repossesses the eternal fullness of its being which envelops then and carries in its grasp the manifold and unified splendours of its nature. At any rate the spiritual process of which our human birth is a step and our life is a portion, appears as the bringing out of a greatness, *asya mahimānam*, which is secret, inherent and self-imprisoned, absorbed in the form and working of things. Our world-action figures an evolution, an outrolling of a manifold Power gathered and coiled up in the crude intricacy of Matter. The upward progress of the successive births of things is a rise into waking and larger and larger light of a consciousness shut into the first hermetic cell of sleep of the eternal Energy.

There is a parallel in the Yogic experience of the Kundalini, eternal Force coiled up in the body in the bottom root vessel or chamber, *mūlādhāra*, pedestal, earth-centre of the physical nervous system. There she slumbers coiled up there like a Python and filled full of all that she holds gathered in her being, but when she is struck by the freely coursing breath, by the current of Life which enters in to search for her, she awakes and rises flaming up the ladder of the spinal chord and forces open centre after centre of the involved dynamic secrets of consciousness till at the summit she finds, joins and becomes one with the spirit. Thus she passes from an involution in inconscience through a series of opening glories of her powers into the greatest eternal superconscience of the spirit. This mysterious evolving Nature in the world around us follows even such a course. Inconscient being is not so much a matrix as a chamber of materialised energy in which are gathered up all the powers of the spirit; they are there, but work in the conditions of the material energy, involved, we say, and therefore not apparent as themselves because they have passed into a form of working subnormal to their own right scale where the characteristics by which we recognise and think we know them are suppressed into a minor and an undetected force of working. As Nature rises in the scale, she liberates them into their recognisable scales of energy, discloses the operations by which they can feel themselves and their greatness. At the highest summit she rises into the self-knowledge of the spirit which informed her action, but because of its involution or concealment in the forms of its workings could not be known in the greatness of its reality. Spirit and Nature discovering the secret of her energies become one at the top of the spiritual evolution by a soul in Nature which awakens to the significance of its own being in the liberation of the highest truth: it comes to know that its births were the births, the assumptions of form of an eternal Spirit, to know itself as that and not a creature of Nature and rises to the possession of the revealed, full and highest power of its own real and spiritual nature. That liberation, because liberation is self-possession, comes to us as the crown of a spiritual evolution.

We must consider all the packed significance of this involution. The spirit involved in material energy is there with all its powers; life, mind and a greater supramental power are involved in Matter. But what do we mean when we say that they are involved, and do we mean that all these things are quite different energies cut off from each other by an essential separateness, but rolled up together in an interaction, or do we mean that there is only one Being with its one energy, varying shades of the light of its power differentiated in the spectrum of Nature? When we say that Life is involved in Matter or in material Force, for of that Force Matter seems after all to be only a various self-spun formation, do we not mean that all this universal working, even in what seems to us its inconscient inanimate action, is a life-power of the spirit busy with formation, and we do not recognise it because it is there in a lower scale in which the characteristics by which we recognise life are not evident or are only slightly evolved in the dullness of the material covering? Material energy would be then Life packed into the density of Matter and feeling out in it for its own intenser recognisable power which it finds within itself in the material concealment and liberates into action. Life itself would be an energy of a secret mind, a mind imprisoned in its own forms and quivering out in the nervous seekings of life for its intenser recognisable power of consciousness which it discovers within the vital and material suppression and liberates into sensibility. No doubt, practically, these powers work upon each other as different energies, but in essence they would be one energy and their interaction the power of the spirit working by its higher on its lower forces, depending on them at first, but yet turning in the scale of its ascent to overtop and master them. Mind too might only be an inferior scale and formulation derived from a much greater and supramental consciousness, and that consciousness too with its greater light and will a characteristic originating power of spiritual being, the power which secret in all things, in mind, in life, in matter, in the plant and the metal and the atom assures constantly by its inevitable action the idea and harmony of the universe. And what is the spirit itself but infinite existence, eternal, immortal being, but always a conscious self-aware being, — and that is the difference between the materialist's mechanical monism and the spiritual theory of the universe, — which here expresses itself in a world finite to our conceptions whose every movement yet bears witness to the Infinite? And this world is because the spirit has the delight of its own infinite existence and the delight of its own infinite self-variation; birth is because all consciousness carries with it power of its own being and all power of being is self-creative and must have the joy of its self-creation. For creation means nothing else than a self-expression; and the birth of the soul in the body is nothing but a mode of its own self-expression. Therefore all things here are expression, form, energy, action of the Spirit; matter itself is but form of spirit, life but power of being of the spirit, mind but working of consciousness of the spirit. All Nature is a display and a play of God, power and action and self-creation of the one spiritual Being. Nature presents to spirit at once the force, the instrument, the medium, the obstacle, the result of his powers, and all these things, obstacles as well as instrument, are the necessary elements for a gradual and developing creation.

But if the Spirit has involved its eternal greatness in the material universe and is there evolving its powers by the virtue of a secret self-knowledge, is disclosing them in a grandiose succession under the self-imposed difficulties of a material form of being, is disengaging them from a first veiling absorbed inconscience of Nature, there is no difficulty in thinking or seeing that this soul shaped into humanity is a being of that Being, that this also has risen out of material involution by increasing self-expression in a series of births of which each grade is a new ridge of the ascent opening to higher powers of the spirit and that it is still arising and will not be for ever limited by the present walls of its birth but may, if we will, be born into a divine humanity. Our humanity is the conscious meeting place of the finite and the infinite and to grow more and more towards that Infinite even in this physical birth is our privilege. This Infinite, this Spirit who is housed within us but not bound or shut in by mind or body, is our own self and to find and be our self was, as the ancient sages knew, always the object of our human striving, for it is the object of the whole immense working of Nature. But it is by degrees of the self-finding that Nature enlarges to her spiritual reality. Man himself is a doubly involved being; most of himself in mind and below is involved in a subliminal conscience or a subconscience; most of himself above mind is involved in a spiritual superconscience. When he becomes conscient in the superconscience, the heights and the depths of his being will be illumined by another light of knowledge than the flickering lamp of the reason can now cast into a few corners; for then the master of the field will enlighten this whole wonderful field of his being, as the sun illumines the whole system it has created out of its own glories. Then only he can know the reality even of his own mind and life and body. Mind will be changed into a greater consciousness, his life will be a direct power and action of the Divinity, his very body no longer this first gross lump of breathing clay, but a very image and body of spiritual being. That transfiguration on the summit of the mountain, divine birth, *divya janma*, is that to which all these births are a long series of laborious steps. An involution of spirit in matter is the beginning, but a spiritual assumption of divine birth is the fullness of the evolution.

East and West have two ways of looking at life which are opposite sides of one reality. Between the pragmatic truth on which the vital thought of modern Europe enamoured of the vigour of life, all the dance of God in Nature, puts so vehement and exclusive a stress and the eternal immutable Truth to which the Indian mind enamoured of calm and poise loves to turn with an equal passion for an exclusive finding, there is no such divorce and quarrel as is now declared by the partisan mind, the separating reason, the absorbing passion of an exclusive will of realisation. The one eternal immutable Truth is the Spirit and without the spirit the pragmatic truth of a self-creating universe would have no origin or foundation; it would be barren of significance, empty of inner guidance, lost in its end, a firework display shooting up into the void only to fall away and perish in mid-air. But neither is the pragmatic truth a dream of the non-existent, an illusion or a long lapse into some futile delirium of creative imagination; that would be to make the eternal Spirit a drunkard or a dreamer, the fool of his own gigantic self-hallucinations. The truths of universal existence are of two kinds, truths of the spirit which are themselves eternal and immutable, and these are the great things that cast themselves out into becoming and there constantly realise their powers and significances, and the play of the consciousness with them, the discords, the musical variations, soundings of possibility, progressive notations, reversions, perversions, mounting conversions into a greater figure of harmony; and of all these things the spirit has made, makes always his universe. But it is himself that he makes in it, himself that is the creator and the energy of creation and the cause and the method and the result of the working, the mechanist and the machine, the music and the musician, the poet and the poem, supermind, mind and life and matter, the soul and Nature.

An original error pursues us in our solutions of our problem. We are perplexed by the appearance of an antinomy; we set soul against Nature, the spirit against his creative energy. But Soul and Nature, Purusha and Prakriti, are two eternal lovers who possess their perpetual unity and enjoy their constant difference, and in the unity abound in the passion of the multitudinous play of their difference, and in every step of the difference abound in the secret sense or the overt consciousness of unity. Nature takes the Soul into herself so that he falls asleep in a trance of union with her absorbed passion of creation and she too seems then to be asleep in the whirl of her own creative energy; and that is the involution in Matter. Above, it may be, the Soul takes Nature into himself so that she falls asleep in a trance of oneness with the absorbed self-possession of the spirit and he too seems to be asleep in the deep of his own self-locked immobile being. But still above and below and around and within all this beat and rhythm is the eternity of the spirit who has thus figured himself in soul and nature and enjoys with a perfect awareness all that he creates in himself by this involution and evolution. The soul fulfils itself in Nature when it possesses in her the consciousness of that eternity and its power and joy and transfigures the natural becoming with the fullness of the spiritual being. The constant self-creation which we call birth finds there the perfect evolution of all that it held in its own nature and reveals its own utmost significance. The complete soul possesses all its self and all Nature.

Therefore all this evolution is a growing of the Self in material nature to the conscious possession of its own spiritual being. It begins with form — apparently a form of Force — in which a spirit is housed and hidden; it ends in a spirit which consciously directs its own force and creates or assumes its own forms for the free joy of its being in Nature. Nature holding her own self and spirit involved and suppressed within herself, an imprisoned master of existence subjected to her ways of birth and action, — yet are these ways his and this spirit the condition of her being and the law of her workings, — commences the evolution: the spirit holding Nature conscious in himself, complete by his completeness, liberated by his liberation, perfected in his perfection, crowns the evolution. All our births are the births of this spirit and self which has become or put forth a soul in Nature. To be is the object of our existence, — there is no other end or object, for the consciousness and bliss of being is the whole beginning and middle and end, as it is that which is without beginning or end. But this means in the steps of the evolution to grow more and more until we grow into our own fullness of self; all birth is a progressive self-finding, a means of self-realisation. To grow in knowledge, in power, in delight, love and oneness, towards the infinite light, capacity and bliss of spiritual existence, to universalise ourselves till we are one with all being, and to exceed constantly our present limited self till it opens fully to the transcendence in which the universal lives and to base upon it all our becoming, that is the full evolution of what now lies darkly wrapped or works half evolved in Nature.

Karma

One finds an unanswerable truth in the theory of Karma, —not necessarily in the form the ancients gave to it, but in the idea at its centre, — which at once strikes the mind and commands the assent of the understanding. Nor does the austerer reason, distrustful of first impressions and critical of plausible solutions, find after the severest scrutiny that the more superficial understanding, the porter at the gateways of our mentality, has been deceived into admitting a tinsel guest, a false claimant into our mansion of knowledge. There is a solidity at once of philosophic and of practical truth supporting the idea, a bedrock of the deepest universal undeniable verities against which the human mind must always come up in its fathomings of the fathomless; in this way indeed does the world deal with us, there is a law here which does so make itself felt and against which all our egoistic ignorance and self-will and violence dashes up in the end, as the old Greek poet said of the haughty insolence and prosperous pride of man, against the very foundation of the throne of Zeus, the marble feet of Themis, the adamantine bust of Ananke. There is the secret of an eternal factor, the base of the unchanging action of the just and truthful gods, *devānāṁ dhruva-vratāni*, in the self-sufficient and impartial law of Karma.

This truth of Karma has been always recognised in the East in one form or else in another; but to the Buddhists belongs the credit of having given to it the clearest and fullest universal enunciation and the most insistent importance. In the West too the idea has constantly recurred, but in external, in fragmentary glimpses, as the recognition of a pragmatic truth of experience, and mostly as an ordered ethical law or fatality set over against the self-will and strength of man: but it was clouded over by other ideas inconsistent with any reign of law, vague ideas of some superior caprice or of some divine jealousy, — that was a notion of the Greeks, — a blind Fate or inscrutable Necessity, Ananke, or, later, the mysterious ways of an arbitrary, though no doubt an all-wise Providence. And all this meant that there was some broken half-glimpse of the working of a force, but the law of its working and the nature of the thing itself escaped the perception, — as indeed it could hardly fail to do, since the mental eye of the West, absorbed by the passion of life, tried to read the workings of the universe in the light of the single mind and life of man; but those workings are much too vast, ancient, unbrokenly continuous in Time and all-pervading in Space, — not in material infinity alone, but in the eternal time and eternal space of the soul's infinity, — to be read by so fragmentary a glimmer. Since the eastern idea and name of the law of Karma was made familiar to the modern mentality, one side of it has received an increasing recognition, perhaps because latterly that mentality had been prepared by the great discoveries and generalisations of Science for a fuller vision of cosmic existence and a more ordered and majestic idea of cosmic Law. It may be as well then to start from the physical base in approaching this question of Karma, though we may find at last that it is from the other end of being, from its spiritual summit rather than its material support that we must look in order to catch its whole significance — and to fix also the limits of its significance.

Fundamentally, the meaning of Karma is that all existence is the working of a universal Energy, a process and an action and a building of things by that action, — an unbuilding too, but as a step to farther building, — that all is a continuous chain in which every one link is bound indissolubly to the past infinity of numberless links, and the whole governed by fixed relations, by a fixed association of cause and effect, present action the result of past action as future action will be the result of present action, all cause a working of energy and all effect too a working of energy. The moral significance is that all our existence is a putting out of an energy which is in us and by which we are made and as is the nature of the energy which is put forth as cause, so shall be that of the energy which returns as effect, that this is the universal law and nothing in the world can, being of and in our world, escape from its governing incidence. That is the philosophical reality of the theory of Karma, and that too is the way of seeing which has been developed by physical Science. But its seeing has been handicapped in the progress to the full largeness of its own truth by two persistent errors, first, the strenuous paradoxical attempt — inevitable and useful no doubt as one experiment of the human reason which had to have its opportunity, but foredoomed to failure — to explain supraphysical things by a physical formula, and a darkening second error of setting behind the universal rule of law and as its cause and efficient the quite opposite idea of the cosmic reign of Chance. The old notion of an unintelligible supreme caprice, — unintelligible it must naturally be since it is the working of an unintelligent Force, — thus prolonged its reign and got admission side by side with the scientific vision of the fixities and chained successions of the universe.

Being is no doubt one, and Law too may be one; but it is perilous to fix from the beginning on one type of phenomena with a predetermined will to deduce from that all other phenomenon however different in its significance and nature. In that way we are bound to distort truth into the mould of our own prepossession. Intermediately at least we have rather to recognise the old harmonious truth of Veda — which also came by this way in its end, its Vedanta, to the conception of the unity of Being, — that there are different planes of cosmic existence and therefore too of our own existence and in each of them the same powers, energies or laws must act in a different type and in another sense and light of their effectuality. First, then, we see that if Karma be a universal truth or the universal truth of being, it must be equally true of the inly-born mental and moral worlds of our action as in our outward relations with the physical universe. It is the mental energy that we put forth which determines the mental effect, — but subject to all the impact of past, present and future surrounding circumstance, because we are not isolated powers in the world, but rather our energy a subordinate strain and thread of the universal energy. The moral energy of our action determines similarly the nature and effect of the moral consequence, but subject too — though to this element the rigid moralist does not give sufficient consideration, — to the same incidence of past, present and future surrounding circumstance. That this is true of the output of physical energy, needs no saying nor any demonstration. We must recognise these different types and variously formulated motions of the one universal Force, and it will not do to say from the beginning that the measure and quality of my inner being is some result of the output of a physical energy translated into mental and moral energies, — for instance, that my doing a good or a bad action or yielding to good or to bad affections and motives is at the mercy of my liver, or contained in the physical germ of my birth, or is the effect of my chemical elements or determined essentially and ultimately by the disposition of the constituent electrons of my brain and nervous system. Whatever drafts my mental and moral being may make on the corporeal for its supporting physical energy and however it may be affected by its borrowings, yet it is very evident that it uses them for other and larger purposes, has a supraphysical method, evolves much greater motives and significances. The moral energy is in itself a distinct power, has its own plane of karma, moves me even, and that characteristically, to override my vital and physical nature. Forms of one universal Force at bottom—or at top—these may be, but in practice they are different energies and have to be so dealt with—until we can find what that universal Force may be in its highest purest texture and initial power and whether that discovery can give us in the perplexities of our nature a unifying direction.

Chance, that vague shadow of an infinite possibility, must be banished from the dictionary of our perceptions; for of chance we can make nothing, because it is nothing. Chance does not at all exist; it is only a word by which we cover and excuse our own ignorance. Science excludes it from the actual process of physical law; everything there is determined by fixed cause and relation. But when it comes to ask why these relations exist and not others, why a particular cause is allied to a particular effect, it finds that it knows nothing whatever about the matter; every actualised possibility supposes a number of other possibilities that have not actualised but conceivably might have, and it is convenient then to say that Chance or at most a dominant probability determines all actual happening, the chance of evolution, the stumblings of a groping inconscient energy which somehow finds out some good enough way and fixes itself into a repetition of the process. If Inconscience can do the works of intelligence, it may not be impossible that chaotic Chance should create a universe of law! But this is only a reading of our own ignorance into the workings of the universe,—just as prescientific man read into the workings of physical law the caprices of the gods or any other name for a sportive Chance whether undivine or dressed in divine glories, whether credited with a pliant flexibility to the prayers and bribes of man or presented with an immutable Sphinx face of stone, —but names only in fact for his own ignorance.

And especially when we come to the pressing needs of our moral and spiritual being, no theory of chance or probability will serve at all. Here Science, physical in her basis, does not help except to point out to a certain degree the effects of my physicality on my moral being or of my moral action on my physicality: for anything else of just illumination or useful purpose, she stumbles and splashes about in the quagmire of her own nescience. Earthquake and eclipse she can interpret and predict, but not my moral and spiritual becoming, but only attempt to explain its phenomena when they have happened by imposing polysyllables and fearful and wonderful laws of pathology, morbid heredity, eugenics and what not of loose fumbling, which touch only the draggled skirts of the lowest psycho-physical being. But here I need guidance more than anywhere else and must have the recognition of a law, the high line of a guiding order. To know the law of my moral and spiritual being is at first and last more imperative for me than to learn the ways of steam and electricity, for without these outward advantages I can grow in my inner manhood, but not without some notion of moral and spiritual law. Action is demanded of me and I need a rule for my action: something I am urged inwardly to become which I am not yet, and I would know what is the way and law, what the central power or many conflicting powers and what the height and possible range and perfection of my becoming. That surely much more than the rule of electrons or the possibilities of a more omnipotent physical machinery and more powerful explosives is the real human question.

The Buddhists' mental and moral law of Karma comes in at this difficult point with a clue and an opening. As Science fills our mind with the idea of a universal government of Law in the physical and outward world and in our relations with Nature, though she leaves behind it all a great unanswered query, an agnosticism, a blank of some other ungrasped Infinite, — here covered by the concept of Chance, — the Buddhist conception too fills the spaces of our mental and moral being with the same sense of a government of mental and moral Law: but this too erects behind that Law a great unanswered query, an agnosticism, the blank of an ungrasped Infinite. But here the covering word is more grandly intangible; it is the mystery of Nirvana. This Infinite is figured in both cases by the more insistent and positive type of mind as an Inconscience, — but material in the one, in the other a spiritual infinite zero, — but by the more prudent or flexible thinkers simply as an unknowable. The difference is that the unknown of Science is something mechanical to which mechanically we return by physical dissolution or *laya*, but the unknown of Buddhism is a Permanent beyond the Law to which we return spiritually by an effort of self-suppression, of self-renunciation and, at the latest end, of self-extinction, by a mental dissolution of the Idea which maintains the law of relations and a moral dissolution of the world-desire which keeps up the stream of successions of the universal action. This is a rare and an austere metaphysics; but to its discouraging grandeur we are by no means compelled to give assent, for it is neither self-evident nor inevitable. It is by no means so certain that a high spiritual negation of what I am is my only possible road to perfection; a high spiritual affirmation and absolute of what I am may be also a feasible way and gate. This nobly glacial or blissfully void idea of a Nirvana, because it is so overwhelmingly a negation, cannot finally satisfy the human spirit, which is drawn persistently to some highest positive and affirmation of itself and only uses negations by the way the better to rid itself of what comes in as an obstacle to its self-finding. To the everlasting No the living being may resign itself by an effort, a sorrowful or a superb turning upon itself and existence, but the everlasting Yes is its native attraction: our spiritual orientation, the magnetism that draws the soul, is to eternal Being and not to eternal Non-Being.

Nevertheless certain essential and needed clues are there in the theory of Karma. And first, there is this assurance, this firm ground on which I can base a sure tread, that in the mental and moral world as in the physical universe there is no chaos, fortuitous rule of chance or mere probability, but an ordered Energy at work which assures its will by law and fixed relation and steady succession and the links of ascertainable cause and effectuality. To be assured that there is an all-pervading mental law and an all-pervading moral law, is a great gain, a supporting foundation. That in the mental and moral as in the physical world what I sow in the proper soil, I shall assuredly reap, is a guarantee of divine government, of equilibrium, of cosmos; it not only grounds life upon an adamant underbase of law, but by removing anarchy opens the way to a greater liberty. But there is the possibility that if this Energy is all, I may only be a creation of an imperative Force and all my acts and becomings a chain of determination over which I can have no real control or chance of mastery. That view would resolve everything into predestination of Karma, and the result might satisfy my intellect but would be disastrous to the greatness of my spirit. I should be a slave and puppet of Karma and could never dream of being a sovereign of myself and my existence. But here there comes in the second step of the theory of Karma, that it is the Idea which creates all relations. All is the expression and expansion of the Idea, *sarvāṇi vijñāna-vijṛmbhitāni*. Then I can by the will, the energy of the Idea in me develop the form of what I am and arrive at the harmony of some greater idea than is expressed in my present mould and balance. I can aspire to a nobler expansion. Still, if the Idea is a thing in itself, without any base but its own spontaneous power, none originating it, no knower, no Purusha and Lord, I may be only a form of the universal Idea and myself, my soul, may have no independent existence or initiation. But there is too this third step that I am a soul developing and persisting in the paths of the universal Energy and that in myself is the seed of all my creation. What I have become, I have made myself by the soul's past idea and action, its inner and outer karma; what I will to be, I can make myself by present and future idea and action. And finally, there is this last supreme liberating step that both the Idea and its Karma may have their origin in the free spirit and by arriving at myself by experience and self-finding I can exalt my state beyond all bondage of Karma to spiritual freedom. These are the four pillars of the complete theory of Karma. They are also the four truths of the dealings of Self with Nature.

Karma and Freedom

The universe in which we live presents itself to our mentality as a web of opposites and contraries, not to say contradictions, and yet it is a question whether there can be in the universe any such thing as an entire opposite or a real contradiction. Good and evil seem to be as opposite powers as well can be and we are apt by the nature of our ethical mind to see the world, at any rate in its moral aspect, as a struggle and tug of war between these eternal opposites, God and devil, Deva and Asura, Ahuramazda, Angrya Mainyu. We hope always that on some as yet hardly conceivable day the one will perish and the other triumph and be convinced of eternity; but actually they are so intertangled that some believe they are here always together like light and shadow and, if at all, then only somewhere beyond this world of action, in some restful and silent eternity is there a release from the anguish of the knot of their intertwining, their bitter constant embrace and struggle. Good comes out of evil and again good itself seems often to turn to evil; the bodies of the wrestling combatants get so mixed and confounded together that to distinguish them the minds of the sages even are perplexed and bewildered. And it would seem sometimes as if this distinction hardly existed except for man and the spirits who urge him, perhaps since he ate of that tree of dual knowledge in the garden; for matter knows it not and life below man troubles itself but little, if at all, with moral differences. And it is said too that on the other side of human being and beyond its struggles is a serenity of the high and universal spirit where the soul transcends sin, but transcends also virtue, and neither sorrows nor repents nor asks "Why have I not done the good and where-fore have I done this which is evil?"[1] because in it all things are perfect and to it all things are pure.

But there is a yet more radical instance of the eventual unreality of opposites. For the sages make too an opposition of the Knowledge and the Ignorance, — *vidyā avidyā, citti acitti,* — on which this question of good and evil seems very intimately to hang. Evil runs behind an ignorant urge of the soul in nature, is itself an ignorant perversion of its will, and the partiality of good is equally

[1] Taittiriya Upanishad.

an affliction of the Ignorance. But when we look closely into the essence of these two things, we find that on one side ignorance seems to be nothing else than an involved or a partial knowledge; it is knowledge wrapped up in an inconscient action or it is knowledge feeling out for itself with the tentacles of mind; and again on the other side knowledge itself appears to be at best a partial knowing and always to have something beyond of which it is ignorant, even its highest and widest splendour a golden outbreak of solar effulgence against the mass of blue-black light of infinity through which we look beyond it to the Ineffable.

Our mind is compelled to think always by oppositions, from the practical validity of which we cannot escape, but which yet seem always in some sort questionable. We get a perception of a law of Karma, the constant unavoidable successions of the acts of energy and its insistent stream of consequences and reactions, the chain of causality, the great mass of past causes behind us from which all future consequence ought infallibly to unroll itself, and by this we try to explain the universe; but then immediately there arises the opposite idea and the challenging problem of liberty. Whence comes this notion of liberty, this divine or this Titanic thirst in man for freedom, born perhaps of something in him by which, however finite be his mind and life and body, he participates in the nature of infinity? For when we look round on the world as it is, everything seems to be by necessity and to move under a leaden constraint and compulsion. This is the aspect of the unthinking world of Force and Matter in which we live; and even in ourselves, in man the thinker, how little is free from some kind of present constraint and of compelling previous necessity! So much of what we are and do is determined by our environment, so much has been shaped by our education and upbringing, — we are made by life and by the hands of others, are clay for many potters: and, as for what is left, was it not determined, even that which is most ourselves, by our individual, our racial, our human heredity or in the last resort by universal Nature who has shaped man and each man to what he is for her blind or her conscient uses?

But we insist and say that we have a will which is aware of a however heavily burdened freedom and can shape to its own purpose and change by its effort environment and upbringing and the formations of heredity and even our apparently immutable common nature. But this will and its effort, is it not itself an instrument, even a mechanical engine of Nature, the active universal energy, and is not its freedom an arbitrary illusion of our mentality which lives in each moment of the present and separates it by ignorance, by an abstraction of the mind from its determining past, so that I seem at every critical moment to exercise a free and virgin choice, while all the time my choice is dominated by its own previous formation and by all that obscure past which I ignore? Granted that Nature works through our will and can create and change, can, that is to say, produce a new formation out of the stuff she has provided for her workings, is it not by a past impulsion and a continuous energy from it that the thing is done? That is the first idea of Karma. Certainly, our present will must come in as one though not by any means the sole element of the act and formation, but in this view it is not a free ever-new will, but in the first place a child and birth of all the past nature, our action, our present karma the result of an already formed shape of the force of that nature, swabhava. And in the second place our will is an instrument constantly shaped and used by something greater than ourselves. Only if there is a soul or self which is not a creation, but a master of Nature, not a formation of the stream of universal energy, but itself the former and creator of its own Karma, are we justified in our claim of an actual freedom or at least in our aspiration to a real liberty. There is the whole heart of the debate, the nodus and escape of this perplexed issue.

But here the critical negative analytic thinker, ancient nihilistic Buddhist or modern materialist, comes in to take away the basis of any actual freedom in our earthly or in any possible heavenly existence. The Buddhist denied the existence of a Self free and infinite; that, he thought, was only a sublimation of the idea of ego, an imposition, *adhyāropa*, or gigantic magnified shadow thrown by the falsehood of our personality on eternal Non-Existence. But as for the soul, there is no soul, but only a stream of forms, ideas and sensations, and as the idea of a chariot is only a name for the combination of planks and pole and wheels and axles, so is the idea of individual soul or ego only a name for the combination or continuity of these things. Nor is the universe itself anything other than such a combination, *saṁhata*, formed and maintained in its continuity by the successions of Karma, by the action of Energy. In this mechanical existence there can be no freedom from Karma, no possible liberty; but there is yet a possible liberation, because that which exists by combination and bondage to its combinations can be liberated from itself by dissolution. The motive power which keeps Karma in motion is desire and attachment to its works, and by the conviction of impermanence and the cessation of desire there can come about an extinction of the continuity of the idea in the successions of Time.

But if this extinction may be called a liberation, it is yet not a status of freedom; for that can only repose upon an affirmation, a permanence, not upon a negative and extinction of all affirmations, and needs too, one would imagine, a someone or something that is free. The Buddha himself, it may be remarked, seems to have conceived of Nirvana as a status of absolute bliss of freedom, a negation of Karmic existence in some incognisable Absolute which he refused steadfastly to describe or define by any positive or any negative, — as indeed definition by any exclusive positive or widest sum of positives or any negative or complete sum of negatives would seem by the very fact of its bringing in a definition and thereby a limitation to be inapplicable to the Absolute. The Illusionist's Maya is a more mystic thing and more obscure to the intelligence; but we have at least here a Self, a positive Infinite which is capable therefore of an eternal freedom, but only in inaction, by cessation from Karma. For the self as the individual, the soul in action of Karma is bound always by ignorance, and only by rejection of individuality and of the cosmic illusion can we return to the liberty of the Absolute. What we see in both these systems is that spiritual freedom and the cosmic compulsion are equally admitted, but in a total separation and an exclusion from each other's own proper field, — still as absolute opposites and contraries. Compulsion of ignorance or Karma is absolute in the world of birth; freedom of the spirit is absolute in a withdrawal from birth and cosmos and Karma.

But these trenchant systems, however satisfactory to the logical reason, are suspect to a synthetic intelligence; and at any rate, as we find that knowledge and ignorance are not in their essence absolute contraries but ignorance and inconscience itself the veil of a secret knowledge, so it may be at least possible that liberty and the compulsion of Karma are not such unbridgeable opposites, but that behind and even in Karma itself there is all the time a secret liberty of the indwelling Spirit. Buddhism and Illusionism too do not assert any external or internal predestination, but only a self-imposed bondage. And very insistently they demand of man a choice between the right and the wrong way, between the will to an impermanent existence and the will to Nirvana, between a will to cosmic existence and the will to an absolute spiritual being. Nor do they demand this choice of the Absolute or of the universal Being or Power, who indeed cares nothing for their claim and goes on very tranquilly and securely with his mighty eternal action, but they ask it of the individual, of the soul of man halting perplexed between the oppositions of his mentality. It would seem then that there is something in our individual being which has some real freedom of will, some power of choice of a great consequence and magnitude, and what is it then that thus chooses, and what are the limits, where the beginning or the end of its actual or its possible liberty?

Difficult also is it to understand how unsubstantial Impermanence can have such a giant hold or present this power of eternal continuity in Time, — there must surely, one thinks, be a Permanent which expresses itself in this continuity, *dhruvam adhruveṣu*; or how an Illusion, — for what is illusion but an inconsequent dream or unsubstantial hallucination? — can build up this mighty world of just sequence and firm law and linked Necessity; some secret self-knowledge and wisdom there must be which guides the Energy of Karma in its idea and has appointed for her the paths she must hew in Time. It is because of their persistence of principle in all the transiences of particular form that things have such a hold on our mind and will. It is because the world is so real that we feel so potently its grasp on us and our spirits turn on it with this grip of the wrestler. It is often indeed too fiercely real for us and we seek for liberty in the realm of dream or planes of the ideal and, not finding it sufficiently there, because we have not the freedom nor can develop the mastery to impose our ideal on this active reality, we seek it beyond in the remote and infinite greatness of the Absolute. We shall do better then to fix on that other more generally admissible distinction, namely, of the world of Karma as a practical or relative reality and the being of the Spirit constant behind it or brooding above it as a greater supreme reality. And then we have to find whether in the latter alone is any touch of freedom or whether, as must surely be if it is the Spirit that presides over the Energy at work and over its action, there is here too some element or some beginning at least

of liberty, and whether, even if it be small and quite relative, we
cannot in these steps of Time, in these relations of Karma make
this freedom great and real by dwelling consciously in the greatness of the Spirit. May not that be the sovereignty we shall find
here when we rise to the top of the soul's evolution?

One thing we will note that this urge towards control and this
impression of freedom are an orientation and an atmosphere
which cling about the action of mind, and they grow in Nature as
she rises towards mentality. The world of Matter seems to know
nothing about freedom; everything there appears as if written in
sibyllic laws upon tablets of stone, laws which have a process, but
no initial reason, serve a harmony of purposes or at least produce a
cosmos of fixed results, but do not appear to be shaped with an eye
to them by any discoverable Intelligence. We can think of no
presence of soul in natural things, because we can see in them no
conscious action of mind and a conscious active mental intelligence
is to our notions the very basis and standing-ground, if not the
whole stuff of soul-existence. If Matter is all, then we may very
easily conclude that all is a Karma of material energy which is
governed by some inherent incomprehensible mechanically
legislating Necessity. But then we see that Life seems to be made
of a different stuff; here various possibility develops, here creation
becomes eager, pressing, flexible, protean; here we are conscious
of a searching and a selection, many potentialities and a choice of
actualities, of a subconscient idea which is feeling around for its
vital self-expression and shaping an instinctive action, — often,
though in certain limits, with an unerring intuitive guidance of life
to its immediate objective or to some yet distant purpose, — of a
subconscient will too in the fibre of all this vast seeking and
mutable impulse. But yet this too works within limits, under
fetters, in a given range of processes.

But when we get out into mind, Nature becomes there much
more widely conscious of possibility and of choice; mind is aware
of potentialities and of determinations in idea which are other than
those of the immediate actuality or of the fixedly necessary consequence of the sum of past and present actualities; it is
aware of numberless "may-be"s and "might-have-been"s, and
these last are not entirely dead rejected things, but can return
through the power of the Idea and effect future determinations
and can fulfil themselves at last in the inner reality of their idea

though, it may well be, in other forms and circumstances. Moreover, mind can and does go still further; it can conceive of an infinite possibility behind the self-limitations of actual existence. And from this seeing there arises the idea of a free and infinite Will, a Will of illimitable potentiality which determines all these innumerable marvels of its own universal becoming or creation in Space and Time. That means the absolute freedom of a Spirit and Power which is not determined by Karma, but determines Karma. Apparent Necessity is the child of the spirit's free self-determination. What affects us as Necessity, is a Will which works in sequence and not a blind Force driven by its own mechanism.

This is not, however, a binding inference and always there remain on this head arguable by the reason three main conceptions which we can form of existence. First, there is the idea, facile to our reason, of a blind mechanical Necessity of some kind, — and against or behind that nothing or some absolute non-existence. The nature of this Necessity would be that of a fixed processus bound to certain initial and general determinations of which all the rest is the consequence. But that is only a first appearance of universal things, the stamp of phenomenal impression which we get from the aspect of the material universe. Then, there is the idea of a free infinite Being, God or Absolute, who somehow or other creates out of something or out of nothing, in reality or only in conception, or brings out of himself into manifestation a world of the necessity of his will or Maya or Karma in which all things, all creatures are bound as the victims of a necessity, not mechanical or external, but spiritual and internal, a force of Ignorance or a force of Karma or else some kind of arbitrary predestination. And, finally, there is the idea of an absolute free Existence which supports, develops and informs a universe of relations, of that Power as the universal Spirit of our existence, of the world as the evolution of these relations, of beings in the universe as souls who work them out with some freedom of the spirit as its basis, — for that they inwardly are, — but with an observation of the law of the relations as their natural condition.

This law would be in phenomenon or as seen in a superficial view of its sole outward machinery an apparent chain of necessity, but in fact it would be a free self-determination of the Spirit in existence. The free self and spirit would be there informing all the action of material energy, secretly conscient in its inconscience; his would be the movement of life and its inner spirit of guidance; but in mind would be something of the first open light of his presence. The soul evolving in Nature, *prakṛtir jīvabhūtā*, would be an immortal clouded Power of him growing into the light of the spirit and therefore towards the consciousness and reality of freedom. It would be bound at first in Nature and obey helplessly in all its action the urge of Karma, because on the surface the action of energy would be whole truth of its kinetic being; the rest, the freedom, the origination is there, but concealed below, subliminal and therefore not at all manifest in the action. Even in mentality the action of Karma would be the main fact; everything would be determined by the nature of force of our active being working upon and responding to the influences of the environment and by the nature of quality of our active being which would colour and shape the character of these out-puttings and responses. But that force is the force, that quality the quality of the soul; and as the soul grew aware of itself, the consciousness of Freedom would emerge, assert itself, insist, strive to grow into a firmly felt and possessed reality. Free in the spirit within, conditioned and determined in Nature, striving in his soul to bring out the spiritual light, mastery and freedom to work upon the obscurity and embarrassment of his first natural conditions and their narrow determinations, this would be the nature of man the mental being.

On this basis it becomes possible to come at some clear and not wholly antinomous relation between man's necessity and man's freedom, between his earthly human nature at whirl in the machinery of mind, life and body and the master Soul, the Godhead, the real Man behind whose consent supports or whose bidding governs its motions. The soul of man is a power of the self-existence which manifests the universe and not the creature and slave of a mechanical Nature; and it is only the natural instruments of his being, it is mind, life and body and their functions and members which are helpless apparatus and gear of the machinery. These things are subject to the action of Karma, but man in himself, the real man within is not its subject, *na karma lipyate nare*. Rather is Karma his instrument and its developments the material he uses, and he is using it always from life to life for the shaping of a limited and individual, which may be one day a divine and cosmic personality. For the eternal spirit enjoys an absolute freedom. This freedom appears to us no doubt in a certain status, origin or background of all being as an unconditioned infinite of existence, but also it is in relation to the universe the freedom of an existence which displays an infinite of possibilities and has a power of shaping at will out of its own potentiality the harmonies of the cosmos. Man, too, may well be capable of a release, *mokṣa*, into the unconditioned Infinite by cessation of all action, mind and personality. But that is not the whole of the spirit's absolute freedom; it is rather an incomplete liberty, since it endures only by its inaction. But the freedom of the Spirit is not so dependent; it can remain unimpaired in all this action of Karma and is not diminished or abrogated by the pouring of its energies into the whirl of the universe. And one may say that man cannot enjoy the double freedom because as man he is an individual being and therefore a thing in Nature, subject to Ignorance, to Karma. To be free he must get away from individuality, nature and Karma, and then man no longer exists, there is only the unconditioned Infinite. But this is to assume that there is no power of spiritual individuality, but only a power of individuation in Nature. All is then a formation of a nodus of mental, vital and physical Karma with which the one self for a long time mistakenly identifies its being by the delusion of ego. But if on the contrary there is any such thing as an individual power of spirit, it must, in whatever degree of actuality share in the united force and freedom of the self-existent Divinity; for it is being of his being.

Freedom somewhere there is in our being and action, and we have only to see how and why it is limited in our outward nature, why here I am at all under any dominion of Karma. I appear to be bound by the law of an outward and imposed energy only because there is separation between my outward nature and my inmost spiritual self and I do not live in that outwardness with my whole being, but with a shape, turn and mental formation of myself which I call my ego or my personality. The cosmic spirit in matter seems itself to be so bound, for the same reason. It has started an outward compressed action, a law and disposition of material energy which must be allowed to unroll its consequences; itself holds back behind and conceals its shaping touch; but still its supporting assent and impulse are there and these come out more into the open as Nature raises herself in the scales of life and mind. Nevertheless, I have to note that even in mind and even in its phenomenon of a conscious will Karma is the first law and there cannot be for me there a complete freedom; there is no such thing as a mental will which is absolutely free. And this is because mind is part of the action of the outward Ignorance, an action which seeks for knowledge but does not possess its full light and power, which can conceive of self and spirit and infinity and reflect them, but not altogether live in them, which can quiver with infinite possibility, but can only deal in a limited half-effective fashion with restricted possibilities. An Ignorance cannot be permitted to have, even if in its nature it could have, free mastery. It would never do for an ignorant mind and will to be given a wide and real freedom; for it would upset the right order of the energy which the Spirit has set at work and produce a most unholy confusion. It must be forced to obey or, if it resists, to bear the reaction of the Law; its partial freedom of a clouded and stumbling knowledge must be constantly overruled both in its action and its result by the law of universal Nature and the will of the seeing universal Spirit who governs the dispositions and consequences of Karma. This constrained overruled action is in patent fact the character of our mental being and action.

But still there is here something which we may call a relative freedom. It does not really belong to our outward mind and will or that shadow of myself which I have put forth in my mental ego; for these things are instruments and they work in the roads of the successions of Karma. But they still feel a power constantly coming forth and either assenting to or intervening in the action of the nature, and that power they attribute to themselves. They are aware of a relative freedom in their disposition of action and of at least a potential absolute freedom behind it, and mixing these two things confusedly together mind, will and ego cry out in unison "I am free." But this freedom and power are influences from the soul. To use a familiar metaphysical language, they type the assent and will of the Purusha without which the Prakriti cannot move on her way. The first and the greater part of this soul-influence is in the form of an assent to Nature, an acquiescence; and for good reason. For I start with the action of the universal Energy which the Spirit has set in motion and as I rise from the ignorance towards knowledge, the first thing demanded from me is to gather experience of its law and of my relations to the law and partly therefore to acquiesce, to allow myself to be moved, to see and to come to know the nature of the motions, to suffer and obey the law, to understand and know Karma.

This obedience is forcibly imposed on the lower ignorant creation. But thinking man who experiences increasingly from generation to generation and from life to life the nature of things and develops reflective knowledge and the sense of his soul in Nature, delivers in her a power of initiating will. He is not bound to her set actualities; he can refuse assent, and the thing in Nature to which it is refused goes on indeed for a time and produces its results by impetus of Karma, but as it runs, it loses power and falls into impotence and desuetude. He can do more, he can command a new action and orientation of his nature. The assent was a manifestation of the power of the soul as giver of the sanction, *anumantā*, but this is a power of the soul as active lord of the nature, *īśvara*. Then Nature still insists more or less on her old habitual way by reason of her past impetus or the right of previous sanctions and may even, in proportion as she is unaccustomed to control, resist and call in hostile powers, our own creations, the children of our past willings; then is there a battle in the house of our being between the lord and his spouse or between old and new nature and a defeat of the soul or its victory. And this is certainly a freedom, but only a relative freedom, and even the greatest mental self-mastery a relative and precarious thing at the best. This liberty when we look down at it from a higher station, is not well distinguishable from a lightened bondage.

The mental being in us can be a learner in the school of freedom, not a perfect adept. A real freedom comes when we get away from the mind into the life of the spirit, from personality to the Person, from Nature to the lord of Nature. There again the first liberty is a passive power; it is of the nature of an assent; it is an observing and essential liberty in which the active part of the being is an instrument of the supreme Spirit and its universal action. But the assent is to the will of the Spirit and not to the mechanical force of Nature, and there is thrown on the mind the freedom of the spirit's light and purity and a right knowledge of relations and a clear detached assent to the divine workings. But if man would have too a freedom of power, of participation, of companionship as the son of God in a greater divine control, he must then not only get back from mind, but must stand, in his thought and will even, above the levels of mentality and find there

a station of leverage, a spiritual *pou sto*,[1] whence he can sove-
reignly move the world of his being. Such a station of consciousness there is in our supramental ranges. When the soul is one with
the Supreme and with the universal not only in essence of
consciousness and spiritual truth of being, but in expressive act too
of consciousness and being, when it enjoys an initiating and
relating truth of spiritual will and knowledge and the soul's
overflowing delight in God and existence, when it is admitted to
the spirit's fullness of assent to self and its creative liberty, its
strain of an eternal joy in self-existence and self-manifestation,
Karma itself becomes a rhythm of freedom and birth a strain of
immortality.[2]

---

[1] A "where to stand," the station of leverage from which Archimedes, could
he only have found it, undertook to move the world.

[2] *sambhūtyā amṛtam aśnute*, "by birth he enjoys immortality."

Karma, Will and Consequence

Will, Karma and consequence are the three steps of the Energy which moves the universe. But Karma and consequence are only the outcome of will or even its forms; will gives them their value and without it they would be nothing, nothing at least to man the thinking and growing soul and nothing, it may be hazarded, to the Spirit of which he is a flame and power as well as a creature. The thing we first see or imagine we see, when we look at the outward mechanism of the universe, is energy and its works, action and consequence. But by itself and without the light of an inhabiting will this working is only a huge soulless mechanism, a loud rattling of crank and pulley, a monstrous pounding of spring and piston. It is the presence of the spirit and its will that gives a meaning to the action and it is the value of the result to the soul that gives its profound importance to all great or little consequence. It would not matter to any one or anything, not even to the cosmos itself, though this universal stir came to an end tomorrow or had never been created, if these suns and systems were not the field of a consciousness which there rolls out its powers, evolves its works, enjoys its creations, plans and exults in its immense aims and sequences. Spirit and consciousness and power of the spirit and Ananda are the meaning of existence. Take away this spiritual significance and this world of energy becomes a mechanical fortuity or a blind and rigid Maya.

The life of man is a portion of this vast significance, and since it is in him that on this material plane it comes out in its full capacity of meaning, a very important and central portion. The Will in the universe works up to him in the creative steps of its energy and makes of his nature a chariot of the gods on which it stands within the action, looks out on its works from the very front and no longer only from behind or above Nature's doings and moves on to the ultimate consequences and the complete evolution of its purpose. The will of man is the agent of the Eternal for the unveiling of his secret meaning in the material creation. Man's mind takes up all the knots of the problem and works them out by the power of the spirit within him and brings them nearer to the full force and degree of their individual and cosmic solutions. This is his dignity and his greatness and he needs no other to justify and give a perfect value to his birth and his acts and his passing and his return to birth, a return which must be — and what is there in it to grieve at or shun? — until the work of the Eternal in him is perfected or the cycles rest from the glory of their labour.

This view of the world is the standpoint from which we must regard the question of man's conscious will and its dealings with life, because then all things fall into their natural place and we escape from exaggerated and depreciated estimates. Man is a conscious soul of the Eternal, one with the Infinite in his inmost being, and the spirit within him is master of his acts and his fate. For fate is *fatum*, the form of act and creation declared beforehand by a Will within him and the universe as the thing to be done, to be achieved, to be worked out and made the self-expression of his spiritual being. Fate is *adṛṣṭa*, the unseen thing which the Spirit holds hidden in the plan of its vision, the consequence concealed from the travailing mind absorbed in the work of the moment by the curtained nearnesses or the far invisible reaches of Time. Fate is *niyati*, the thing willed and executed by Nature, who is power of the Spirit, according to a fixed law of its self-governed workings. But since this Eternal and Infinite, our greater Self, is also the universal being, man in the universe is inseparably one with all the rest of existence, not a soul working out its isolated spiritual destiny and nature while all other beings are nothing but his environment and means or obstacles, — that they are indeed, but they are much more to him, — which is the impression cast on the mind by the thought or the religions that emphasise too much his centre of individuality or his aim of personal salvation. He is not indeed solely a portion of the universe. He is an eternal soul which, though limited for certain temporal purposes in its outward consciousness, has to learn to enlarge itself out of those limits, to find and make effective its unity with the eternal Spirit who informs and transcends the universe. That spiritual necessity is the truth behind the religious dogma.

But also he is one in God and one in Nature with all beings in the cosmos, touches and includes all other souls, is linked to all powers of the Being that are manifest in this cosmic working. His soul, thought, will, action are intimate with the universal soul, thought, will and action. All acts on and through him and mixes with him and he acts too on all and his thought and will and life mix in and become a power of the one common life. His mind is a form and action of the universal mind. His call is not to be busy and concerned only with his own growth and perfection and natural destiny or spiritual freedom. A larger action too claims him. He is a worker in a universal work; the life of others is his life; world-consequence and the world-evolution are also his business. For he is one self with the selves of all other beings.

The dealings of our will with Karma and consequence have to be envisaged in the light of this double truth of man's individuality and man's universality. And seen in this light the question of the freedom of our individual will takes on another appearance. It becomes clear enough that our ego, our outward personality can be only a minor, a temporal, an instrumental form of our being. The will of the ego, the outward, the mentally personal will which acts in the movement cannot be free in any complete or separate sense of freedom. It cannot so be free because it is bound by its partial and limited nature and it is shaped by the mechanism of its ignorance, and again because it is an individualised form and working of the universal energy and at every moment impinged upon and modified and largely shaped by environing wills and powers and forces. But also it cannot so be free because of the greater Soul in us behind the mind which determines works and consequence according to the will in its being and the nature, its power of being, not in the moment but in the long continuities of Time, not solely by the immediate adaptation to the environment, but by its own previous intention which has shaped the environment and already predetermined in great part the present act and consequence. The inward will in the being which is in intimacy with that Power is the real will and this outward thing only an instrumentation for a working out from moment to moment, a spring of the karmic mechanism. That inward will we find when we get back to it, to be a free will, not armoured in a separate liberty, but free in harmony with the freedom of the Spirit guiding and compelling Nature in all souls and in all happenings. This thing our outward mind cannot see easily because the practical truth which it feels is the energy of Nature at once working on us from without and forming too our action from within and reacting upon herself by the mental will, her instrument, to continue her self-shaping for farther Karma and farther consequence. Yet are we aware of a self and the presence of this self imposes on our minds the idea of someone who wills, someone who shapes even the nature and is responsible for consequence.

To understand one must cease to dwell exclusively on the act and will of the moment and its immediate consequences. Our present will and personality are bound by many things, by our physical and vital heredity, by a past creation of our mental nature, by environmental forces, by limitation, by ignorance. But our soul behind is greater and older than our present personality. The soul is not the result of our heredity, but has prepared by its own action and affinities this heredity. It has drawn around it these environmental forces by past karma and consequence. It has created in other lives the mental nature of which now it makes use. That ancient soul of long standing, sempiternal in being, *puruṣaḥ purāṇaḥ sanātanaḥ*, has accepted the outward limitation, the outward ignorance as a means of figuring out in a restriction of action from moment to moment the significance of its infinity and the sequence of its works of power. To live in this knowledge is not to take away the value and potency of the moment's will and act, but to give it an immensely increased meaning and importance. Then each moment becomes full of things infinite and can be seen taking up the work of a past eternity and shaping the work of a future eternity. Our every thought, will, action carries with it its power of future self-determination and is too a help or a hindrance for the spiritual evolution of those around us and a force in the universal working. For the soul in us takes in the influences it receives from others for its own self-determination and gives out influences which the soul in them uses for their growth and experience. Our individual life becomes an immensely greater thing in itself and is convinced too of an abiding unity with the march of the universe.

And karma and consequence also get a wider meaning. At present we fix too much on the particular will and act of the moment and a particular consequence in a given time. But the particular only receives its value by all of which it is a part, all from which it comes, all to which it moves. We fix too much also on the externalities of karma and consequence, this good or that bad action and result of action. But the real consequence which the soul is after is a growth in the manifestation of its being, an enlarging of its range and action of power, its comprehension of delight of being, its delight of creation and self-creation, and not only its own but the same things in others with which its greater becoming and joy are one. Karma and consequence draw their meaning from their value to the soul; they are steps by which it moves towards the perfection of its manifested nature. And even when this object is won, our action need not cease, for it will keep its value and be a greater force of help for all these others with whom in self we are one. Nor can it be said that it will have no self-value to the soul grown aware of freedom and infinity; for who shall persuade me that my infinity can only be an eternal full stop, an endless repose, an infinite cessation? Much rather should infinity be eternally capable of an infinite self-expression.

The births of the soul are the series of a constant spiritual evolution, and it might well seem that when the evolution is finished, and that must be, it might at first appear, when the soul involved in ignorance returns to self-knowledge, the series of our births too ought to come to a termination. But that is only one side of the matter, one long act here of the eternal drama, doing, karma. The spirit we are is not only an eternal consciousness and eternal being; its characters are an eternal power of being and an eternal Ananda. Creation is not to the spirit a trouble and an anguish, but a delight expressed, even though in the entirety of its depths inexpressible, fathomless, endless, inexhaustible. It is only the limited action of mind in the ignorance straining after possession and discovery and unable to find the concealed power of the spirit that makes of the delight of action and creation a passion or suffering: for, limited in capacity and embarrassed by life and body, it has yet desires beyond its capacity, because it is the instrument of a growth and the seed of an illimitable self-expression and it has the pain of the growth and the pain of the obstacle and the pain of the insufficiency of its action and delight. But let this struggling self-creator and doer of works once grow into the consciousness and power of the secret infinite spirit within it and all this passion and suffering passes away into an immeasurable delight of liberated being and its liberated action.

The Buddhist perception of karma and suffering as inseparable, that which drove the Buddha to the search for a means of the extinction of the will to be, is only a first phase and partial appearance. To find self is the cure of suffering, because self is infinite possession and perfect satisfaction. But to find self in quiescence is not the whole meaning of the spiritual evolution, but to find it too in its power of being; for being is not only eternal status, but also eternal movement, not only rest, but also action. There is a delight of rest and a delight of action, but in the wholeness of the spirit these two things are no longer contraries, but one and inseparable. The status of the spirit is an eternal calm, but also its self-expression in world-being is without any beginning or end, because eternal power means an eternal creation. When we gain the one, we need not lose its counterpart and consequence. To get to a foundation is not to destroy all capacity for superstructure.

Karma is nothing but the will of the Spirit in action, consequence nothing but the creation of will. What is in the will of being, expresses itself in karma and consequence. When the will is limited in mind, karma appears as a bondage and a limitation, consequence as a reaction or an imposition. But when the will of the being is infinite in the spirit, karma and consequence become instead the joy of the creative spirit, the construction of the eternal mechanist, the word and drama of the eternal poet, the harmony of the eternal musician, the play of the eternal child. This lesser, bound, seemingly separate evolution is only a step in the free self-creation of the Spirit from its own illimitable Ananda. That is behind all we are and do; to hide it from mind and bring it slowly forward into the front of existence and action is the present play of Self with Nature.

Rebirth and Karma

The ancient idea of Karma was inseparably connected with a belief in the soul's continual rebirth in new bodies. And this close association was not a mere accident, but a perfectly intelligible and indeed inevitable union of two related truths which are needed for each other's completeness and can with difficulty exist in separation. These two things are the soul side and the nature side of one and the same cosmic sequence. Rebirth is meaningless without karma, and karma has no fount of inevitable origin and no rational and no moral justification if it is not an instrumentality for the sequences of the soul's continuous experience. If we believe that the soul is repeatedly reborn in the body, we must believe also that there is some link between the lives that preceded and the lives that follow and that the past of the soul has an effect on its future; and that is the spiritual essence of the law of Karma. To deny it would be to establish a reign of the most chaotic incoherence, such as we find only in the leaps and turns of the mind in dream or in the thoughts of madness, and hardly even there. And if this existence were, as the cosmic pessimist imagines, a dream or an illusion or, worse, as Schopenhauer would have it, a delirium and insanity of the soul, we might accept some such law of inconsequent consequence. But, taken even at its worst, this world of life differs from dream, illusion and madness by its plan of fine, complex and subtle sequences, the hanging together and utility even of its discords, the general and particular harmony of its relations, which, if they are not the harmony we would have, not our longed-for ideal harmony, has still at every point the stamp of a Wisdom and an Idea at work; it is not the act of a Mind in tatters or a machine in dislocation. The continuous existence of the soul in rebirth must signify an evolution if not of the self, for that is said to be immutable, yet of its more outward active soul or self of experience. This evolution is not possible if there is not a connected sequence from life to life, a result of action and experience, an evolutionary consequence to the soul, a law of Karma.

And on the side of Karma, if we give to that its integral and not a truncated meaning, we must admit rebirth for the sufficient field of its action. For Karma is not quite the same thing as a material or substantial law of cause and effect, the antecedent and its mechanical consequence. That would perfectly admit of a Karma which could be carried on in time and the results come with certainty in their proper place, their just degree by a working out of the balance of forces, but need not in any way touch the human originator who might have passed away from the scene by the time the result of his acts got into manifestation. A mechanical Nature could well visit the sins of the fathers not on them, but on their fourth or their four-hundredth generation, as indeed this physical Nature does, and no objection of injustice or any other mental or moral objection could rise, for the only justice or reason of a mechanism is that it shall work according to the law of its structure and the fixed eventuality of its force in action. We cannot demand from it a mind or a moral equity or any kind of supraphysical responsibility. The universal energy grinds out inconsciently its effects and individuals are only fortuitous or subordinate means of its workings; the soul itself, if there is a soul, makes only a part of the mechanism of Nature, exists not for itself, but as an utility for her business. But Karma is more than a mechanical law of antecedent and consequence. Karma is action, there is a thing done and a doer and an active consequence; these three are the three joints, the three locks, the three *sandhis* of the connexus of Karma. And it is a complex mental, moral and physical working; for the law of it is not less true of the mental and moral than of the physical consequence of the act to the doer. The will and the idea are the driving force of the action, and the momentum does not come from some commotion in my chemical atoms or some working of ion and electron or some weird biological effervescence. Therefore the act and consequence must have some relation to the will and the idea and there must be a mental and moral consequence to the soul which has the will and idea. That, if we admit the individual as a real being, signifies a continuity of act and consequence to him and therefore rebirth for a field of this working. It is evident that in one life we do not and cannot labour out and exhaust all the values and powers of that life, but only carry on a past thread, weave out something in the present, prepare infinitely more for the future.

   This consequence of rebirth would not follow from the very nature of Karma if there were only an All-Soul of the universe. For then it would be that which is carrying on in myriads of forms its past, working out some present result, spinning yarn of karma for a future weft of consequence. It is the All-Soul which would be the originator, would upbear the force of the act, would receive and exhaust or again take up for farther uses the returning force of the consequence. Nothing essential would depend on its doing all these things through the same individual mask of its being. For the individual would only be a prolonged moment of the All-Soul, and what it originated in this moment of its being which I call myself, might very well produce its result on some other moment of the same being which from the point of view of my ego would be somebody quite different from and unconnected with myself. There would be no injustice, no unreason in such an apparently vicarious reaping of the fruit or suffering of the consequence; for what has a mask, though it be a living and suffering mask, to do with these things? And, in fact, in the nature of life in the material universe a working out of the result of the action of one in the lives of many others, an effect of the individual's action on the group or the whole is everywhere the law. What I sow in this hour, is reaped by my posterity for several generations and we can then call it the karma of the family. What the men of today as community or people resolve upon and execute, comes back with a blessing or a sword upon the future of their race when they themselves have passed away and are no longer there to rejoice or to suffer; and that we can speak of as the karma of the nation. Mankind as a whole too has a karma; what it wrought in its past, will shape its future destiny; individuals seem only to be temporary units of human thought, will, nature who act according to the compulsion of the soul in humanity and disappear; but the karma of the race which they have helped to form continues through the centuries, the millenniums, the cycles.

But we can see, when we look into ourselves, that this relation of the individual to the whole has a different significance; it does not mean that I have no existence except as a more or less protracted moment in the cosmic becoming of the All-Soul: that too is only a superficial appearance and much subtler and greater is the truth of my being. For the original and eternal Reality, the Alpha and Omega, the Godhead is neither separate in the individual nor is he only and solely a Pantheos, a cosmic spirit. He is at once the eternal individual and the eternal All-Soul of this and many universes, and at the same time he is much more than these things. This universe might end, but he would still be; and I too, though the universe might end, could still exist in him; and all these eternal souls would still exist in him. But as his being is for ever, so the succession of his creations too is for ever; if one creation were to come to an end, it would be only that another might begin and the new would carry on with a fresh commencement and initiation the possibility that had not been worked out in the old, for there can be no end to the self-manifestation of the Infinite. *Nāsti anto vistarasya me.* The universe finds itself in me, even as I find myself in the universe, because we are this face and that face of the one eternal Reality, and individual being is as much needed as universal being to work out this manifestation. The individual vision of things is as true as the universal vision, both are ways of the self-seeing of the Eternal. I may now see myself as a creature contained in the universe; but when I come to self-knowledge, I see too the universe to be a thing contained in myself, subtly by implication in my individuality, amply in the great universalised self I then become. These are data of an ancient experience, things known and voiced of old, though they may seem shadowy and transcendental to the positive modern mind which has long pored so minutely on outward things that it has become dazed and blind to any greater light and is only slowly recovering the power to see through its folds; but they are for all that always valid and can be experienced today by any one of us who chooses to turn to the deepest way of the inner experience. Modern thought and science, if we look at the new knowledge given us in its whole, do not contradict them, but only trace for us the outward effect and workings of these realities; for always we find in the end that truth of self is not contradicted, but reproduced and made effectual here by law of Energy and law of Matter.

The necessity of rebirth, if we look at it from the outward side, from the side of energy and process, stands upon a persistent and insistent fact which supervenes always upon the generality of common law and kind and constitutes the most intimate secret of the wonder of existence, the uniqueness of the individual. And this uniqueness is everywhere, but appears as a subordinate factor only in the lower ranges of existence. It becomes more and more important and pronounced as we rise in the scale, enlarges in mind, gets to enormous proportions when we come to the things of the spirit. That would seem to indicate that the cause of this significant uniqueness is something bound up with the very nature of spirit; it is something it held in itself and is bringing out more and more as it emerges out of material Nature into self-conscience. The laws of being are at bottom one for all of us, because all existence is one existence; one spirit, one self, one mind, one life, one energy of process is at work; one will and wisdom has planned or has evolved from itself the whole business of creation. And yet in this oneness there is a persistent variety, which we see first in the form of a communal variation. There is everywhere a group energy, group life, group mind, and if soul is, then we have reason to believe that however elusive it may be to our seizing, there is a group-soul which is the support and foundation — some would call it the result — of this communal variety. That gives us a ground for a group karma. For the group or collective soul renews and prolongs itself and in man at least develops its nature and experience from generation to generation. And who knows whether, when one form of it is disintegrated, community or nation, it may not wait for and assume other forms in which its will of being, its type of nature and mentality, its attempt of experience is carried forward, migrates, one might almost say, into new-born collective bodies, in other ages or cycles? Mankind itself has this separate collective soul and collective existence. And on that community the community of karma is founded; the action and development of the whole produces consequence of karma and experience for the individual and the totality even as the action and development of the individual produces consequences and experience for others, for the group, for the whole. And the individual is there; you cannot reduce him to a nullity or an illusion; he is real, alive, unique. The communal soul-variation mounts up from the rest, exceeds, brings in or brings out something more, something new, adds novel powers in the evolution. The individual mounts and exceeds in the same way from the community. It is in him, on his highest heights that we get the flame-crest of self-manifestation by which the One finds himself in Nature.

And the question is how does that come about at all? I enter into birth, not in a separate being, but in the life of the whole, and therefore I inherit the life of the whole. I am born physically by a generation which is a carrying on of its unbroken history; the body, life, physical mentality of all past being prolongs itself in me and I must therefore undergo the law of heredity; the parent, says the Upanishad, recreates himself by the energy in his seed and is reborn in the child. But as soon as I begin to develop, a new, an independent and overbearing factor comes in, which is not my parents nor my ancestry, nor past mankind, but I, my own self. And this is the really important, crowning, central factor. What matters most in my life, is not my heredity; that only gives me my opportunity or my obstacle, my good or my bad material, and it has not by any means been shown that I draw all from that source. What matters supremely is what I make of my heredity and not what my heredity makes of me. The past of the world, bygone humanity, my ancestors are there in me; but still I myself am the artist of my self, my life, my actions. And there is the present of the world, of humanity, there are my contemporaries as well as my ancestors; the life of my environment too enters into me, offers me a new material, shapes me by its influence, lays its direct or its indirect touch on my being. I am invaded, changed, partly recreated by the environing being and action in which I am and act. But here again the individual comes in subtly and centrally as the decisive power. What is supremely important is what I make of all this surrounding and invading present and not what it makes of me. And in the interaction of individual and general Karma in which others are causes and produce an effect in my existence and I am a cause and produce an effect on them, I live for others, whether I would have it so or no, and others live for me and for all. Still the central power of my psychology takes its colour from this seeing that I live for my self, and for others or for the world only as an extension of my self, as a thing with which I am bound up in some kind of oneness. I seem to be a soul, self or spirit who constantly with the assistance of all create out of my past and present my future being and myself too help in the surrounding creative evolution.

What then is this all-important and independent power in me and what is the beginning and the end of its self-creation? Has it, even though it is something independent of the physical and vital present and past which gives to it so much of its material, itself no past and no future? Is it something which suddenly emerges from the All-Soul at my birth and ceases at my death? Is its insistence on self-creation, on making something of itself for itself, for its own future and not only for its fleeting present and the future of the race, a vain preoccupation, a gross parasitical error? That would contradict all that we see of the law of the world-being; it would not reduce our life to a greater consistency with the frame of things, but would bring in a freak element and an inconsistency with the pervading principle. It is reasonable to suppose that this powerful independent element which supervenes and works upon the physical and vital evolution, was in the past and will be in the future. It is reasonable also to suppose that it did not come in suddenly from some unconnected existence and does not pass out after one brief intervention; its close connection with the life of the world is rather a continuation of a long past connection. And this brings in at once the whole necessity of past birth and karma. I am a persistent being who pursue my evolution within the persistent being of the world. I have evolved my human birth and I help constantly in the human evolution. I have created by my past karma my own conditions and my relations with the life of others and the general karma. That shapes my heredity, my environment, my affinities, my connections, my material, my opportunities and obstacles, a part of my predestined powers and results, not arbitrarily predestined but predetermined by my own stage of nature and past action, and on this groundwork I build new karma and farther strengthen or subtilise my power of natural being, enlarge experience, go on with my soul evolution. This process is woven in with the universal evolution and all its lines are included in the web of being, but it is not merely a jutting point or moment of it or a brief tag shot into the tissue. That is what rebirth means in the history of my manifested self and of universal being.

The old idea of rebirth errs on the contrary by an excessive individualism. Too self-concentrated, it treated one's rebirth and karma as too much one's own single affair, a sharply separate movement in the whole, leaned too much on one's own concern with one's self and even while it admitted universal relations and a unity with the whole, yet taught the human being to see in life principally a condition and means of his own spiritual benefit and separate salvation. That came from the view of the universe as a movement which proceeds out of something beyond, something from which each being enters into life and returns out of it to its source, and the absorbing idea of that return as the one thing that at all matters. Our being in the world, so treated, came in the end to be regarded as an episode and in sum and essence an unhappy and discreditable episode in the changeless eternity of the Spirit. But this was too summary a view of the will and the ways of the Spirit in existence. Certain it is that while we are here, our rebirth or karma, even while it runs on its own lines, is intimately one with the same lines in the universal existence. But my self-knowledge and self-finding too do not abolish my oneness with other life and other beings. An intimate universality is part of the glory of spiritual perfection. This idea of universality, of oneness not only with God or the eternal Self in me, but with all humanity and other beings, is growing to be the most prominent strain in our minds and it has to be taken more largely into account in any future idea or computation of the significance of rebirth and karma. It was admitted in old time; the Buddhist law of compassion was a recognition of its importance; but it has to be given a still more pervading power in the general significance.

The self-effectuation of the Spirit in the world is the truth on which we take our foundation, a great, a long self-weaving in time. Rebirth is the continuity of that self-effectuation in the individual, the persistence of the thread; Karma is the process, a force, a work of energy and consequence in the material world, an inner and an outer will, an action and mental, moral, dynamic consequence in the soul evolution of which the material world is a constant scene. That is the conception; the rest is a question of the general and particular laws, the way in which karma works out and helps the purpose of the spirit in birth and life. And whatever those laws and ways may be, they must be subservient to this spiritual self-effectuation and take from it all their meaning and value. The law is a means, a line of working for the spirit, and does not exist for its own sake or for the service of any abstract idea. Idea and law of working are only direction and road for the soul's progress in the steps of its existence.

Karma and Justice

What are the lines of Karma? What is the intrinsic character and active law of this energy of the soul and its will and development of consequence? To ask that question is to ask what is the form taken here by the dynamic meaning of our existence and what the curves of guidance of its evolving self-creation and action. And such a question ought not to be answered in a narrow spirit or under the obsession of some single idea which does not take into account the manysidedness and rich complexity of this subtle world of Nature. The law of Karma can be no rigid and mechanical canon or rough practical rule of thumb, but rather its guiding principle should be as supple a harmonist as the Spirit itself whose will of self-knowledge it embodies and should adapt itself to the need of self-development of the variable individual souls who are feeling their way along its lines towards the right balance, synthesis, harmonics of their action. The karmic idea cannot be — for spirit and not mind is its cause — a cosmic reflection of our limited average human intelligence, but rather the law of a greater spiritual wisdom, a means which behind all its dumb occult appearances embodies an understanding lead and a subtle management towards our total perfection.

The ordinary current conception of law of Karma is dominantly ethical, but ethical in no very exalted kind. Its idea of karma is a mechanical and materialistic ethics, a crudely exact legal judgment and administration of reward and punishment, an external sanction to virtue and prohibition of sin, a code, a balance. The idea is that there must be a justice governing the award of happiness and misery on the earth, a humanly intelligible equity and that the law of Karma represents it and gives us its formula. I have done so much good, *puṇya*. It is my capital, my accumulation and balance. I must have it paid out to me in so much coin of prosperity, the legal currency of this sovereign and divine Themis, or why on earth should I at all do good? I have done so much evil. That too must come back to me in so much exact and accurate punishment and misfortune. There must be so much outward suffering or an inward suffering caused by outward event and pressure; for if there were not this physically sensible, visible, inevitable result, where would be any avenging justice and where could we find any deterrent sanction in Nature against evil? And this award is that of an exact judge, a precise administrator, a scrupulous merchant of good for good and evil for evil who has learned nothing and will never learn anything of the Christian or Buddhistic ideal rule, has no bowels of mercy or compassion, no forgiveness for sin, but holds austerely to an eternal Mosaic law, eye for eye, tooth for tooth, a full, slow or swift, but always calm and precisely merciless *lex talionis*.

This commercial and mathematical accountant is sometimes supposed to act with a startling precision. A curious story was published the other day, figuring as a fact of contemporary occurrence, of a rich man who had violently deprived another of his substance. The victim is born as the son of the oppressor and in the delirium of a fatal illness reveals that he has obliged his old tyrant and present father to spend on him and so lose the monetary equivalent of the property robbed minus a certain sum, but that sum must be paid now, otherwise — The debt is absolved and as the last pice is expended, the reborn soul departs, for its sole object in taking birth is satisfied, accounts squared and the spirit of Karma content. That is the mechanical idea of Karma at its acme of satisfied precision. At the same time the popular mind in its attempt to combine the idea of a life beyond with the notion of rebirth, supposes a double prize for virtue and a double penalty for transgression. I am rewarded for my good deeds in heaven after death until the dynamic value of my virtue is exhausted and I am then reborn and rewarded again materially on earth. I am punished in hell to the equivalence of my sins and again punished for them in another life in the body. This looks a little superfluous and a rather redundant justice, and, even, the precise accountant becomes very like an unconscionable hundred per cent usurer. Perhaps it may be said that beyond earth it is the soul that suffers — for purification, and here the physical being — as a concession to the forces of life and the symmetry of things: but still it is the soul that thus pays double in its subtle experience and in its physical incarnation.

The strands of our nature which mix in this natural but hardly philosophic conception, have to be disentangled before we can disengage the right value of these ideas. Their first motive seems to be ethical, for justice is an ethical notion; but true ethics is dharma, the right fulfilment and working of the higher nature, and right action should have right motive, should be its own justification and not go limping on the crutches of greed and fear. Right done for its own sake is truly ethical and ennobles the growing spirit; right done in the lust for a material reward or from fear of the avenging stripes of the executioner or sentence of the judge, may be eminently practical and useful for the moment, but it is not in the least degree ethical, but is rather a lowering of the soul of man; or at least the principle is a concession to his baser animal and unspiritual nature. But in natural man, born before the higher dharma and more potent and normal as a motive to action, come two other very insistent things, *kāma*, *artha*, desire and pleasure of enjoyment with its corresponding fear of suffering, and interest of possession, acquisition, success with its complementary pain of lacking and frustration, and this is what governs most prominently the normal barbaric or still half barbaric natural man. He needs to some not small extent if he is to conform his close pursuit of desire and interest to the ethical standard, a strict association or identity of result of virtue with some getting of his interest and pleasure and result of sin with some loss of materially or vitally desirable things and the infliction of mental, vital or physical pain. Human law proceeds on this principle by meeting the grosser more obvious offences with punishment and avenging pain or loss and on the other hand assuring the individual in some degree of the secure having of his legitimate pleasure and interest if he observes the legal rule. The cosmic law is expected by the popular theory of Karma to deal with man on his own principle and do this very thing with a much sterner and more unescapable firmness of application and automatic necessity of consequence.

The cosmic Being must be then, if this view is to hold, a sort of enlarged divine Human or, we might say, a superior anthropoid Divine, or else the cosmic Law a perfection and magnitude of human methods and standards, which deals with man as he is accustomed to deal with his neighbour, — only not with a rough partial human efficacy, but either a sure omniscience or an unfailing automatism. Whatever truth there may be behind that notion, this is not likely to be an adequate account of the matter. In actual life, if we put aside the rebirth theory, there are traces of this method, but it does not work out with any observable consistency, — not even if we accept an unsatisfactory and hardly just vicarious punishment as part of the scheme. What surety have we, then, of its better or its faultless working out in rebirth except for some similar partial signs and indications and, to fill in the blanks, our general sense of the fitness of things? And again where does the true nature of ethics come in in this scheme? That more elevated action, it would almost seem, is an ideal movement of less use for the practical governance of life than as one part of a preparation for a fourth and last need of man, his need of spiritual salvation, and salvation winds up finally our karma and casts away the economy along with the very thought and will of life. Desire is the law of life and action and therefore of Karma. To do things above the material level for their own sake and their pure right or pure delight is to head straight towards the distances of heaven or the silence of the Ineffable. But this is a view of the meaning of existence against which it is time for the higher seeing mind and being of man to protest and to ask whether the ways of the Spirit in the world may not be capable of a greater, nobler and wiser significance.

But still, since the mind of man is part of the universal mind and reflects something of it in a however broken or as yet imperfect and crookedly seeing fashion, there may well be something of a real truth behind this view, though it is not likely to be the whole or the well understood truth. There are some certain or probable laws of the universal working which are relevant to it and must enter into the account. First, it is sure that Nature has laws of which the observance leads to or helps well-being and of which the violation imposes suffering; but all of them cannot be given a moral significance. Then there is the certainty that there must be a moral law of cause and consequence in the total web of her weaving and this we would perhaps currently put into the formula that good produces good and evil evil, which is a proposition of undoubted truth, though also we see in this complicated world that evil comes out of what we hold to be good, and again out of evil disengages itself something that yet turns to good. Perhaps our system of values is too rigidly precise or too narrowly relative; there are subtle things in the totality, minglings, interrelations, cross-currents, suppressed or hidden significances which we do not take into account. The formula is true, but is not the whole truth, at least as now understood in its first superficial significance.

And at any rate in the ordinary notion of Karma we are

combining two different notions of good. I can well understand that moral good does or ought to produce and increase moral good and moral evil to farther and to create moral evil. It does so in myself. The habit of love confirms and enhances my power of love; it purifies my being and opens it to the universal good. The habit of hatred on the contrary corrupts my being, fills it with poison, with bad and morbid toxic matter, and opens it to the general power of evil. My love ought also by a prolongation or a return to produce love in others and my hatred to give rise to hatred; that happens to a certain, a great extent, but it need not be and is not an invariable or rigorous consequence; still we may well see and believe that love does throw out widening ripples and helps to elevate the world while hatred has the opposite consequence. But what is the necessary connection between this good and evil on the one hand and on the other pleasure and pain? Must the ethical power always turn perfectly into some term of kindred hedonistic result? Not entirely; for love is a joy in itself, but also love suffers; hatred is a troubled and self-afflicting thing, but has too its own perverse delight of itself and its gratifications; but in the end we may say that love, because it is born of the universal Delight, triumphs in its own nature and hatred because it is its denial or perversion, leads to a greater sum of misery to myself as to others. And of all true moral good and real evil this may be said that the one tends towards some supreme Right, the *ṛtam* of the Vedic Rishis, the highest law of a highest Truth of our being and that Truth is the door of the spirit's Ananda, its beatific nature, the other is a missing or perversion of the Right and the Truth and exposes us to its opposite, to false delight or suffering. And even in the perplexed steps of life some reflection of this identity must emerge.

This correspondence is, still, more essentially true in the inner field, in the spiritual, mental and emotional result and reaction of the good or the evil or of the effects of its outgoing action. But where is the firm link of correspondence between the ethical and the more vital and physical hedonistic powers of life? How does my ethical good turn into smiling fortune, crowned prosperity, sleek material good and happiness to myself and my ethical evil into frowning misfortune, rugged adversity, sordid material ill and suffering, — for that is what the desire soul of man and the intelligence governed by it seem to demand, — and how is the account squared or the transmutation made between these two very different energies of the affirmation and denial of good? We can see this much that the good or the evil in me translates itself into a good or an evil action which among other things brings about much mental and material happiness and suffering to others, and to this outgoing power and effect there ought to be an equal reaction of incoming power and effect, though it does not seem to work itself out immediately or with any discoverable exactness of correspondence. There does still appear to be a principle of rebound in Nature; our action has in some degree the motion of recoil of the boomerang and cycles back towards the will that has cast it on the world. The stone we hurl rashly against the universal Life is cast back at us and may crush, maim or injure our own mental and physical being. But this mechanical rebound is not the whole principle of Karma. Nor is Karma wholly a mixed ethical-hedonistic order in its total significance, for there are involved other powers of our consciousness and being. Nor is it again a pure mechanism which we set going by our will and have then helplessly to accept the result; for the will which produced the effect, can also intervene to modify it. And above all the initiating and receiving consciousness can change the values and utilities of the reactions and make another thing of life than this automatic mechanism of fateful return or retribution to the half-blind embodied actor in a mute necessity of rigorous law of Nature.

The relation of our consciousness and will to Karma is the thing upon which all the subtler lines of action and consequence must depend; that connexus must be the hinge of the whole significance. The dependence of the pursuit of ethical values on a sanction by the inferior hedonistic values, material, vital and lower mental pleasure, pain and suffering, appeals strongly to our normal consciousness and will; but it ceases to have more than a subordinate force and finally loses all force as we grow towards greater heights of our being. That dependence cannot then be the whole or the final power or guiding norm of Karma. The relation of will to action and consequence must be cast on more subtle and liberal lines. The universal Spirit in the law of Karma must deal with man in the lower scale of values only as a part of the transaction and as a concession to man's own present motives. Man himself puts these values, makes that demand for pleasure and prosperity and dreads their opposites, desires heaven more than he loves virtue, fears hell more than he abhors sin, and while he does so, the world-dispensation wears to him that meaning and colour. But the spirit of existence is not merely a legislator and judge concerned to maintain a standard of legal justice, to dole out deterrents and sanctions, rewards and penalties, ferocious pains of hell, indulgent joys of paradise. He is the Divine in the world, the Master of a spiritual evolution and the growing godhead in humanity. That godhead grows however slowly beyond the dependence on the sanctions of pleasure and pain. Pain and pleasure govern our primary being and in that primary scale pain is Nature's advertisement of things we should avoid, pleasure her lure to things she would tempt us to pursue. These devices are first empirical tests for limited objects; but as I grow, I pass beyond their narrower uses. I have continually to disregard Nature's original warnings and lures in order to get to a higher nature. I have to develop a nobler spiritual law of Karma.

This will be evident if we consider our own greater motives of action. The pursuit of Truth may entail on me penalties and sufferings; the service of my country or the world may demand from me loss of my outward happiness and good fortune or the destruction of my body; the increase of my strength of will and greatness of spirit may be only possible by the ardours of suffering and the firm renunciation of joys and pleasures. I must still follow after Truth, I must do the service to my race my soul demands from me; I must increase my strength and inner greatness and must not ask for a quite irrelevant reward, shun penalty or make a bargain for the exact fruits of my labour. And that which is true of my action in the present life, must be equally true of my connected action and self-development through many births. Happiness and sorrow, good fortune and ill-fortune are not my main concern whether in this birth or in future lives, but my perfection and the higher good of mankind purchased by whatever suffering and tribulation. Spinoza's dictum that joy is a passage to a greater perfection and sorrow a passage to a lesser perfection is a much too summary epigram. Delight will be indeed the atmosphere of perfection and attends too even the anguish of our labour towards it, but first a higher delight which has often much trouble for its price, and afterwards a highest spiritual Ananda which has no dependence on outward circumstances, but rather is powerful to new-shape their meanings and transform their reactions. These things may be above the first formulation of the world energy here, may be influences from superior planes of the universal existence, but they are still a part of the economy of Karma here, a process of the spiritual evolution in the body. And they bring in a higher soul nature and will and action and consequence, a higher rule of Karma.

The law of Karma is therefore not simply an extension of the human idea of practical justice into future births and a rectification there of the apparent injustice of life. A justice or rather a justness there must be in all the workings of the world-energy; Nature certainly seems to be scrupulous in her measures. But in the life of man there are many factors to be taken into the reckoning; there are too stages, grades, degrees. And on a higher step of our being things do not look the same nor are quite the same as on a lower grade. And even in the first normal scale there are many factors and not only the ethical-hedonistic standard. If it is just that the virtuous man should be rewarded with success and happiness and the wicked man punished with downfall and pain at some time, in some life, on earth or in heaven or in hell, it is also just that the strong man should have the reward of his cultivated strength, the intellectual man the prize of his cultivated skill, the will that labours in whatever field the fruit of its effort and its works. But it does not work rightly, you say, not morally, not according to the ethical law? But what is right working in this connection of will and action and consequence? I may be religious and honest, but if I am dull, weak and incompetent? And I may be selfish and impious, but if I have the swift flame of intellect, the understanding brain, the skill to adapt means to ends, the firm courageous will fixed on its end? I have then an imperfection which must impose its consequences, but also I have powers which must make their way. The truth is that there are several orders of energy and their separate characteristic working must be seen, before their relations can be rightly discovered in the harmonies of Nature. A complex web is what we have to unravel. When we have seen the parts in the whole, the elements and their affinities in the mass, then only can we know the lines of Karma.

THE LINES OF KARMA

The Foundation

The idea of Karma has behind it two ideas that are its constituent factors, a law of Nature, of the energy or action of Nature, and a soul that lives under that law, puts out action into that energy and gets from it a return in accordance and measure with the character of its own activities. And here certain considerations have at once intervened which it will not do to ignore. This putting out of action and its return cannot have anything more than a mechanical importance, it cannot have a mental, moral and spiritual significance, if the action of universal Nature is something quite different from the soul's action in character, in meaning, in the law of her being that constitutes it, if it is not itself the energy, the work of a Mind, a Soul, a Spirit. If the individual energy is that of a soul putting out action and receiving a return in kind, physical, mental, moral and spiritual from the universal energy, the universal energy too that makes the return should be that of an All-Soul in which and in relation to which this individual flame of the All-Soul lives. And it is apparent, if we consider, that the individual's energy of action is not something miraculously separate and independent, it is not a power born of itself, living in itself, acting in its separate and wholly self-formed puissance. On the contrary it is the universal that acts in the individual energy and acts, no doubt with an individual application, but on universal lines and in harmony with its universal law. But if that were all the truth, then there would be no real individual and no responsibility of any kind except the responsibility of universal Nature to carry out the idea or to execute the force put forth in the individual as in the universal by the All-Soul, the cosmic Spirit. But there is also this soul of the individual, and that is a being of the Infinite and a conscious and efficient portion of the All-Soul, a deputy or representative, and puts forth the energy given to it according to its own potentiality, type, limits with a will that is in some sense its own. The Spirit in the cosmos is the lord, the Ishwara of all Nature, but the individual soul is likewise a representative, a delegate Ishwara, the underlord at least if not the overlord of his nature, — the recipient, agent and overseer, let us say, of his own form and use of the universal energy of Nature.

And next we see that each being is actually in life, in the world an individual in a species and each species has a nature of its own, á Swabhava or way of the self-being, and each individual too a nature of his own, an individual way of his self-being within that of the species. The law of the action is determined generally by this swabhava of the species and individually by the swabhava of the individual but within that larger circle. Man is at once himself, in a certain way peculiar and unique, and a depressed portion of God and a natural portion of mankind. There is in other words a general and an individual Swadharma or natural principle and law of all action for the kind and for the individual in the kind. And it is clear too that every action must be a particular application, a single result, a perfect or imperfect, right or perverted use of the general and within it of the individual swadharma.

But again, if that were all, if each man came into life with his present nature ready determined for him and irrevocable and had to act according to it, there would be no real responsibility; for he would do good according to the good and evil according to the evil in his nature, he would be imperfect according to its imperfection or perfect according to its perfection; and he might have to suffer the return of his good or evil, bear exactly the just consequences of his perfection or his imperfection, but mechanically and not by his choice: for his apparent choice would be the compulsion of the nature in him and could not be in any way, directly or indirectly, the result of his spirit's will. But in fact there is within his being a power of development, a power of change, or in the language of our modern conceptions an evolutionary power. His nature is what it is because he has so made it by his past; he has induced this present formulation by a precedent will in his spirit. He has risen to humanity by the force of his spirit and by the power of the All-Soul out of the vast possibilities of universal Nature. He has developed by his own long evolution of that humanity the character and law of action of his present individual being; he has built his own height and form of human nature. He may change what he has made, he may rise even, if that be within the possibilities of the universe, beyond human and to or towards superhuman nature. It is the possibility of the universal Nature and her law that determines his natural being and action, but it is part of her law to be subject to the spirit, and she will develop in reply to an insistent call; for then she must respond, she must supply the needed energy, she must determine the acts in that direction, she must assure its issue. His past and his present nature and the environment he has secured may present constant obstacles, but they must still yield in the end to the evolutionary will in him in proportion to its sincerity, wholeness and insistence. All the possibility of the All-being is in him, all the power of the All-Will is behind him. This evolution and all its circumstances, his life, its form, its events, its values arise out of that urge and are shaped according to the past, present or future active will of his spirit. As is his use of the energy, so was and will be the return of the universal energy to him now and hereafter. This is the fundamental meaning of Karma.

At the same time this action and evolution of the spirit taking birth in a body are not an easy and simple thing, as it would or might be if Nature were all of one piece and evolution were only a raising of the degrees of a single power. For there are many strands, many degrees, many forms of energy of Nature. There is in the world of birth an energy of physical being and nature, arising out of the physical an energy of vital being and nature, arising out of the vital an energy of mental being and nature, arising out of the mental an energy of spiritual or supramental being and nature. And each of these forms of energy has a law of its own, lines of its own action, a right to its own manner of operation and existence, because each is fundamental to some necessity of the whole. And we see accordingly that each in its impulse follows its own lines regardless of the rest, each in the combination imposes as much of its domination as it can on the others. The mental being is itself a most complex thing and has several forms of energy, an intellectual, a moral, an emotional, a hedonistic energy of mental nature, and the will in each is in itself absolute for its own rule and is yet forced to be modified in action by the running into it and across it of the other strands. The way and the movement of the world action are indeed a difficult and entangled process, *gahanā karmaṇo gatiḥ*, and therefore too the way and movement of our own action which we cannot separate in its law, however much the mere mind in us might like to have it so, from the law of the world action. And if all these energies are forms of energy of the nature of the Spirit, then it is likely that only when we rise into the consciousness of the supreme spiritual being can we hope wholly to understand all the integral secret and harmony of the world action and therefore the integral meaning and law of Karma.

It may therefore serve a partial purpose but can be of little eventual advantage to try to cut the knot of the riddle by reducing to the law of one form of energy alone all the apparent tangle of the cosmic action. The universe is not solely an ethical proposition, a problem of the antinomy of the good and the evil; the Spirit of the universe can in no way be imagined as a rigid moralist concerned only with making all things obey the law of moral good, or a stream of tendency towards righteousness attempting, hitherto with only a very poor success, to prevail and rule, or a stern Justicer rewarding and punishing creatures in a world that he has made or has suffered to be full of wickedness and suffering and evil. The universal Will has evidently many other and more supple modes than that, an infinity of interests, many other elements of its being to manifest, many lines to follow, many laws and purposes to pursue. The law of the world is not this alone that our good brings good to us and our evil brings evil, nor is its sufficient key the ethical-hedonistic rule that our moral good brings to us happiness and success and our moral evil brings to us sorrow and misfortune. There is a rule of right in the world, but it is the right of the truth of Nature and of the truth of the spirit, and that is a vast and various rule and takes many forms that have to be understood and accepted before we can reach either its highest or its integral principle.

The will in the intellectual being may erect knowledge and truth of knowledge as the governing principle of the Spirit, the will in the volitional being may see Will or Power as very God, the will in the aesthetic being enthrone beauty and harmony as the sovereign law, the will in the ethical being have a vision of it as Right or Love or Justice, and so on through a long chapter. But even though all these may very well be supreme aspects of the Supreme, it will not do to shut up the acts of the Infinite into one formula. And for a beginning it is best to phrase the law of Karma as generally and vaguely as may be and put it simply thus without any particular colour or content that according to the energy put forth shall be its return, not with any mathematical precision of conscious will and its mechanical consequences, but subject to the complicated working of many world forces. If we thus state broadly our foundation, the simplicity of the ordinary solutions disappears, but that is a loss only to love of dogma or to the mind's indolence. The whole law of the cosmic action or even the one law governing all the others cannot well be the measure of a physical, mechanical and chemical energy, nor the law of a life force, nor a moral law or law of mind or of idea forces; for it is evident that none of these things by its single self covers or accounts for all the fundamental powers. There is likely to be something else of which all these are the means and energies. Our initial formula itself can be only a general mechanical rule, but still it is likely to be the practical rule of all parts of the mechanism, and if it only states itself and does at first nothing more, yet an impartial regard on the variety of its operations may open out many meanings and may lead us to the essential significance.

The practical and the efficient base of Karma is all the relation of the soul to the energies of Nature, the use by Purusha of Prakriti. It is the soul's demand on, consent to or use of the energies of Nature and the return and reflex of her energies on the soul that must determine the steps of our progress in our births, whether that progress be in a given direction or a long up and down or in a perpetual circle. There is another, a circumstantial aspect of the law of Karma and that hinges on the turn of our action not only to our self, but to others. The nature of the energies we put forth and even the return and reflex of their consequence upon us affects not only ourselves but all around us and we must account too for the direction of our acts upon others, its effect upon them and the return of the direction and rebound of consequence of the effect upon our own life and being. But the energy we put forth on others is ordinarily of a mixed character, physical, vital, moral, mental and spiritual, and the return and consequence too are of a mixed character. A physical action, a vital pressure thrown forth from ourselves carries in it a mental or moral as well as a physical and vital power and issues often quite beyond our conscious will and knowledge and the consequence to ourselves and to others is found to be different enough in character and measure from anything we intended or could have calculated and foreseen. The calculation escapes us because too complex by far is the universal energy acting through us and our conscious will intervenes in it simply as an instrument; our real acceptance is that of a more fundamental power within, a secret, a subliminal assent of our subconscient and superconscient spirit. And the return too, whatever the agents, is of the same complex universal energy and determined by some difficult correlation of the force acting and the force acted upon in her.

But there is another, an ultimate and essential sense of Karma, a relation in it between the soul in us and the Supreme or the All-Self; on that all is founded and to that all leads and must refer to it at every step. That relation too is not so simple a thing as is imagined by the religions. For it must answer to a very vast spiritual sense underlying the whole process of Karma and there must be a connection of each of our workings in the use of the universal energy to that fundamental and perhaps infinite significance. These three things, the will of the soul in Nature and the action of Nature in and on the soul and through it and back to it, the effect of the intercrossing between the action of the soul on others and the return to it of the force of its action complicated by theirs, and the meaning of the soul's action in relation to its own highest Self and the All-Self, to God, make up between them all the bearings of Karma.

The Terrestrial Law

A consideration of the lines of Karma ought certainly to begin with a study of the action of the world as it is, as a whole, however contrary it may be to the rule or to the desire of our moral or our intellectual reason, and to see if we cannot find in its own facts its own explanation. If the actual truth of the world breaks out from the too rigid cadres our moral sense or our intelligence would like to see imposed on the freely or the inevitably self-determining movement of the Infinite, on the immeasurable largeness of his being or the mighty complexities of his will, it is very likely that that is because our moral sense and our intellect, since they are mental and human, are too narrow to understand or to bind him. Any shifting of the base of the problem by which we get out of the difficulty, impose our limits on what overpasses us and compel God to be even as ourselves, may very well be an evasion and an intellectual device and not the way of truth. The problem of knowledge is after all this, to reflect the movements of the Infinite and see, and not to force it into a mould prepared for it by our intelligence.

The ordinary idea of Karma follows this latter unsound method. The world we see is to our notions, if not immoral, yet non-moral and contradictory to our idea of what it should be. Therefore we go behind it, discover that this earth life is not all, erect anew there our moral rule and rejoice to find that after all the universe does obey our human conceptions and therefore all is well. The mysterious conflict, the Manichean struggle, the inextricable tangle here of good and evil is not cured or accounted for, but we say that at least the good and the evil are justly dealt with according to their kind, this duly rewarded and that duly punished in other worlds or other births, there is therefore a dominant moral law and we may cherish a faith that the good will prevail, Ahuramazda conquer and not Ahriman, and on the whole all is as it should be. Or if not, if the tangle is inextricable, if this world is evil or existence itself an enormous mistake — as it must be, man is inclined to think, if it does not suit his desires and conceptions, — then at least I individually by satisfying the moral law may get out of the tangle away to the pleasures of a better world or to the bodiless and mindless peace of Nirvana.

But the question is whether this is not a rather childish and impatient mood and whether these solutions come anywhere near solving the whole complexity of the problem. Let us grant that a dominant moral law governs, not action, — for that is either free or, if not free, compelled to be of all kinds, — but the result of action in the world and that a supreme good will work itself out in the end. The difficulty remains why that good should use evil as one and almost the chief of its means or the dominant moral law, sovereign, unescapable, categorical, imperative, the practical governor, if not the reason of our existence, should be compelled to fulfil itself through so much that is immoral and by the agency of a non-moral force, through hell on earth and hell beyond, through petty cruelty of punishment and huge fury of avenging calamity, through an immeasurable and, as it seems, never ending sequence of pain and suffering and torture. It must surely be because there are other things in the Infinite and therefore other laws and forces here and of these the moral law, however great and sovereign to itself, has to take account and is compelled to accommodate its own lines to their curve of movement. And if that is so our plain course, if we are to see the true connections, is to begin by studying the separate law and claim of these other forces: for till it is done we cannot know rightly how they act upon and condition or are acted upon and utilised by any moral rule that we may distinguish intervening in the complex of the world action. And first let us look at the terrestrial law as it is apart from any question of rebirth, the joining, the play, the rule, the intention of the forces here: for it may be that the whole principle is already there and that rebirth does not so much correct or change as complete its significance.

But on earth the first energy is the physical; the lines of the physical energy creating the forms, deploying the forces of the material universe are the first apparent conditions of our birth and create the practical basis and the original mould of our earthly existence. And what is the law of this first energy, its self-nature, swabhava and swadharma? It is evidently not moral in the human sense of the word: the elemental gods of the physical universe know nothing about ethical distinctions, but only the bare literal rule of energy, the right track and circuit of the movement of a force, its right action and reaction, the just result of its operation.

There is no morality, no hesitation of conscience in our or the world's elements. The fire is no respecter of persons and if the saint or the thinker is cast into it, it will not spare his body. The sea, the stormwind, the rock on which the ship drives do not ask whether the just man drowned in the waters deserved his fate. If there is a divine or a cosmic justice that works in these cruelties, if the lightning that strikes impartially tree or beast or man, is — but it would appear in the case of the man alone, for the rest is accident, — the sword of God or the instrument of Karma, if the destruction wrought by the volcano, the typhoon or the earthquake is a punishment for the sins of the community or individually of the sins in a past life of each man there that suffers or perishes, at least the natural forces know it not and care nothing about it and rather they conceal from us in the blind impartiality of their rage all evidence of any such intention. The sun shines and the rain falls on the just and the unjust alike; the beneficence and the maleficence of Nature, the gracious and dreadful Mother, her beauty and terror, her utility and her danger are bestowed and inflicted without favour or disfavour on all her children and the good man is no more her favourite than the sinner. If a law of moral punishment is imposed through the action of her physical forces, it must be by a Will from above her or a Force acting unknown to her in her inconscient bosom.

But such a Will could not be itself that of a moral Being ethical after the conceptions of man, — unless indeed it resembled man in his most coldly pitiless and savage moral reason or unreason. For its action involves terrors of punishment that would be abhorred as atrocities in an all-powerful human ruler and could not be other than monstrous in a moral Divine Ruler. A personal God so acting would be a Jehovah-Moloch, a merciless and unrighteous demander of righteousness and mercy. On the other hand an inconscient Force mechanically executing an eternal ethical rule without an author or mover would be a paradox: for morality is a creation of conscious mind; an inconscient machinery could have no idea of good and evil, no moral intention or significance. An impersonal or omni-personal conscious Will or Spirit in the universe could well enact such a law and assure its execution, but must then be, although imposing on us good and evil and their results, itself beyond good and evil. And what is this but to say that the universal Being escapes from our ethical limitations and is a supramoral, appearing to us here in physical Nature as an infra-moral, Infinite?

Now that a conscious Infinite is there in physical Nature, we are assured by every sign, though it is a consciousness not made or limited like ours. All her constructions and motions are those of an illimitable intuitive wisdom too great and spontaneous and mysteriously self-effective to be described as an intelligence, of a Power and Will working for Time in eternity with an inevitable and forecasting movement in each of its steps, even in those steps that in their outward or superficial impetus seem to us inconscient. And as there is in her this greater consciousness and greater power, so too there is an illimitable spirit of harmony and beauty in her constructions that never fails her, though its works are not limited by our aesthetic canons. An infinite hedonism too is there, an illimitable spirit of delight, of which we become aware when we enter into impersonal unity with her; and even as that in her which is terrible is a part of her beauty, that in her which is dangerous, cruel, destructive is a part of her delight, her universal Ananda. If then all else in us, our intelligence, our dynamic and volitional, our aesthetic, our hedonistic being, when they regard the physical universe, feel intuitively the satisfaction in it of something great and illimitable but still mysteriously of their own kind, must not our moral sense, our sense of Right, find too there the satisfaction of something of which it is itself the reflection? An intuitive perception of this kind is at the root of our demand for a moral order in the universe. Yes, but here too our partial conceptions, our own moral canons are not sufficient; this is a greater and illimitable Right, not bound to the ethical formula, and its first principle is that each thing should observe the law of its own energy and each energy move in its own lines in the total scheme and fulfil its own function and make its own returns. The physical law is the right and justice, the duty, the ought of the physical world. The godhead of Fire in the Upanishad, questioned by the Spirit, "What is the power in thee?" makes answer "This is my power that whatever is cast to me, I burn," and a similar answer is made by each physical thing to the question of the life and the mind. It observes the lines of its physical energy and is concerned with no other law or justice. No law of Karma, the moral law included, could exist, if there were not to begin with this principle as the first foundation of order.

What then is the relation of man to this physical Nature, man this soul intervening in and physically born of her in a body subjected to her law of action? what his function as something that is yet more than her, a life and a mind and a spirit? what his swabhava, his swadharma? First, he owes to her a mechanical obedience of which she herself working in his body takes care: but also, as a soul evolving the power of consciousness secret in her, his business is to know and to use her law and even in knowing and using it to transcend her more material limit, habit, purpose and formula. Observance of Nature but also transcendence of first nature is continually the purpose of the Spirit within him. A continuous series of transcendences is the most significant thing in the world action and evolution itself is only Nature's constant impulse and effort of self-exceeding, of a greater self-becoming, her way of expressing more and more, getting out a greater form of birth and awakened power of presence of the self that is in her. Life brings in a whole range of these transcendences, mind another and greater range, and since mind is so evidently imperfect and incomplete, a thing of seeking in its very nature, there must surely be a range or many ranges of transcendence above mind. Man meets with the powers of his mind the rule of the physical action and the law of vital Karma, brings in a law of mental and moral Karma and lifts along the ladder of these scales to something more, to a potency of spiritual action which may even lead him to an exceeding of Karma itself, a freedom from or of birth and becoming, a perfecting transcendence.

Man's exceeding of the physical law does not come solely by his evolution of a moral sense in a non-moral world of Nature. Its essential rule is rather a turning of a conscious intelligence and will on life and matter,— morality itself only this knowledge and will seeking for a rule of truth and right of action, *satyam ṛtam*, in his relation to his inner self and to his fellow beings. But his dealings with the purely physical lines of Nature are non-moral, a matter at first of observance where he must, of satisfaction by instinctive or experienced utilisings, of suffering at her hands by compulsion, and more and more, as he grows, of a struggle of his knowledge and will to know and master her forces for his use and pleasure, for instruments and expedients, for a greater base and circle of opportunities, for the joy itself of will and knowledge. He makes her forces his opportunities and to increase them faces her perils.

He defies her powers, transgresses her limitations, sins constantly against her first prohibitions, takes her punishments and overcomes them, becomes by wrestling of his mind and will with her acquainted with her greater possibilities which she herself has left unused while she waited for his coming. She meets his effort with physical obstruction and opposition, with a No that constantly recedes, with the mask of his own ignorance, with the menace of her danger. One might suggest the fancy, — attributing to her that resistance which certain instincts in man oppose to the daring of spiritual adventure, to new enlargings of knowledge, new forms of will or new standards of conduct, regarding them stupidly as sin and impiety because they transgress what is established, — that to physical Nature in her first power life itself with its starts and deviations and stumblings and sufferings is a sin against her law of sure physical harmony and exact measure and much more mind with its daring, its sin of boundless adventure, its final yearnings towards the unmeasured, the above-law, the infinite.

But in fact all that the godhead of physical Nature is concerned with in man's dealings with her is to observe a just law of return of her energies to his effort. Wherever his knowledge and will can harmonise itself with the lines of her energies, she makes a return according to its action on her: where it works on her with insufficiency, ignorance, carelessness, error, she overwhelms his effort or injures; as he wills more and discovers more, she returns to him a greater utility and fruit of her powers, consents to his masteries and favours his violences. He has arrived at a unity, a Yoga with her in her greater secret possibilities, — he has liberated them and, as he uses them, so he has from her their return. He observes and he extends for her her lines and she responds with an exact ministry and obedience. All this he can do at present within certain physical limits and lines of working and there is a modification but not a radical change. There are indications that by a more direct pressure of a mental and psychical energy on the physical, the response can be made more variable, the physical depart from what seem to be fixed limits and habits, and it is conceivable that as knowledge and will entered into the region of higher and yet higher powers, the action of physical energy might grow entirely responsive, giving whatever return is seemingly demanded from her, and its lines perfectly flexible. But even this transcendence would have to regard the great original measures fixed by the All-Will: there could be a free use, perhaps a large transformation of the physical energy, but not a departure from its fundamental law and purpose.

All this founds a reign of law, a principle of the just return of energy that is the neutral essence of Karma, but it has no eye of regard for ethical measures and no moral significance. Man may and does invent cruel and immoral means of getting at physical knowledge and its powers or turn to unethical ends the energies she places at his service, but that is a matter between his will and his own soul and of his relation with other living beings, his and their concern and not hers. Physical Nature gives impartially her results and rewards and demands from man observance not of the moral but the physical law: she asks for a just knowledge and a scrupulous practice of her physical lines and nothing else. There is no karmic retort from her on the many cruelties of science, no revolt against an unethical use of her facilities, much punishment of ignorance but none of wickedness. If there is something in the lower rounds of Nature which reacts against certain transgressions of the moral law, it begins obscurely on a higher scale, with life. A vital reaction of the kind there is and it produces physico-vital effects, but mark that in this kind of reaction there is no obser-vance of our limits and measures, but rather the same promiscuous impartiality as in the acts of physical Nature. In this field we have to admit a law of vicarious punishment, a constant smiting of the innocent for the sins of the guilty which would seem shocking and brutally unethical and unjust to us if inflicted by a human being. Life seems to punish itself for its errors and excesses without any care to limit the reaction to the agent of the excess or the error. There is here an order of the lines of energy that is not at least primarily or in intention ethical, but rather concerned with a system of returns not governed by our moral ideas.

The movements of life seem indeed to be as little as the physical laid on ethical lines. The fundamental right and justice of life is to follow the curve of the vital energies, to maintain the functions of the life force and to give a return to its own powers. Its function is to survive, to reproduce itself, to grow and possess and enjoy, to prolong and enlarge and assure its action, power, having, pleasure as much as earth will allow. All means are good to life that secure these ends: the rest is a matter of right balance between the vital energy and its physical means, of a putting forth of its powers and the kind of return it gets for those powers. At first — and this continues even after the emergence of mind in life and as long as mind is subservient to the life force, — that is all we see. Vital nature works out her ends faultlessly enough, but not by any means blamelessly in the ethical sense. Death is her second means of self-preservation, destruction her constant instrument for change and renovation and progress, suffering inflicted on oneself or on others oftenest her price for victory and pleasure. All life lives upon other life, makes a place for itself by encroachment and exploitation, possesses by association but even more by struggle. Life acts by mutual shock and mutual use of creatures by each other; but it works only partly by mutual help and very much by a mutual assault and devouring. And its reproduction is bound to a means that the ethical sense even when most tolerant feels to be animal and inferior, is inclined to regard as immoral in itself and, when raised to its ascetic or puritan acuities, rejects as vile. And yet when once we put aside our limited human conceptions and look with impersonal eyes on this vast and various and wonderful vital nature into which we are born, we find in it a mysteriously perfect order, the work of a deep and illimitable intuitive wisdom, an immense Power and will at its perfectly seeing work, a great whole of beauty and harmony built out of what seems to us a system of discords, a mighty joy of life and creation which no heaviest toll of individual death or suffering can tire or discourage and which, when we enter into oneness with the great Ananda of its movement, these things seem rather to cast into relief and against the hue of its ecstasy these shades not to matter. There is here also, in these steps of vital Nature and the law of her energies, a truth of the infinite; and this truth of the Infinite's insistence on life, life as it were for its own sake and for the joy of creation has its own standards of right and harmony, just balance and measure, fit action and reaction of energy that cannot be judged by the human rule. It is a pre-mental and still impersonal Tapas and Ananda and therefore a still non-moral order.

Man's relation with vital Nature is, again, first to be one with it by observance and obedience to its rule, then to know and direct it by conscious intelligence and will and to transcend by that direction the first law of life, its rule and habit, formula, initial significance. At first he is compelled to obey its instincts and has to act even as the animal, but in the enlarged terms of a mentalised impulsion and an increasingly clear consciousness and responsible will in what he does. He too has first to strive to exist, to make a place for himself and his kind, to grow and possess and enjoy, to prolong, to enlarge and assure the first vital lines of his life movement. He too does it even as the others, by battle and slaughter, by devouring, by encroachment, by laying his yoke on earth and her products and on her brute children and on his fellowmen. His virtue, his dharma of the vital nature, *virtus*, *aretē*, is at first an obligation to strength and swiftness and courage and all things that make for survival, mastery and success. Most even of the things in him that evolve an ethical significance have at root not a truly ethical but a dynamic character, — such as self-control, *tapasyā*, discipline. They are vital-dynamic, not ethical energies; they are a rightly massed and concentrated, rightly ordered putting forth of mentalised life forces and the return they seek and get are of the vital and dynamic kind, power, success, mastery, increased capacities of vital possession and expansion or the result of these things, vital-hedonistic, the satisfaction of his desires, vital happiness, enjoyment and pleasure.

Man's first business is to bring his conscious intelligence and will to enlarge the lines of life of the individual and the race. Here again it is to these two powers primarily and only secondarily and partially to any moral force that the life energy gives its returns. The battle in life's primitive values is to the strong and the race to the swift, and the weak and the torpid cannot claim the goal and the crown on the strength of their greater virtue; and there is in this a justice, while the moral principle of reward would be here an injustice, for it would be a denial of the principle of the right returns of energy which is fundamental to any possible law of Karma. Raise the action by the powers of the mind and still the greater successes, the glory and the victory, fall to the men of great intelligence and the men of great will and not necessarily to the more ethical intelligence or to the more moralised will. Morality counts in this dynamic aspect of life only as a prudential check or a concentrating tapasya. Life helps those who most wisely and faithfully follow her impulses while observing her limits and restraints or those who most powerfully aid her greater impulses of expansion. It is those that get the most prudential profit out of her and these the most of her power and movement and joy.

The greater movement at the same time brings in a power of

greater suffering as well as joy, the greater sins of life and its greater virtues. Man as he dares the perils of physical nature, dares too the perils of the vital energy by transgressing her safe rules and limits which she imposes automatically on the animal. There are balances of her use of her energies, safe measures and restraints which make living as secure as it can be, — for all living is naturally a peril and an adventure, but a certain prudence in Nature minimises the adventure as much as is consistent with her ends and the intelligence of man tries to do still better, to live securely and not dangerously, to exclude the more formidable incertitudes from the order of his life. But the instinct of expansion in man is continually breaking Nature's vital balances and disregarding his own limits and measures. He is avid of experience, of the unmeasured and unknown in power and experience and enjoyment as of the common and known and safe, of the perilous extremes as of the sane averages. He must sound all life's possibilities, test the wrong as well as the right use of her energies, pay his toll of suffering and get his prize of more splendid victories. As far as mind working in life's ways can do it, he has to enlarge the lines of life and to make a transformation of its action and its possibilities. This has hitherto been a greatening of forms and never gone so far as to make a radical change and override its first nature. It is only by a transformation of our inner life that we can get beyond the magnified, mentalised, reasoning and consciously willing animal that for the most part the greater number of us are and only by raising it up to unity with some spiritual power we have not yet reached that we can hope to transform vital nature and make her a free instrument of the higher spirit. Then man may be really what he strives to be, master of his life, in control of vital and physical Nature.

Meanwhile it is through an inward turn of his mind that he gets to something like a transcendence, a living not for life but for truth, for beauty, for power of the soul, for good and right, love, justice. It is this endeavour that brings down into the lower rounds of energy the powers of a higher circle, something of a mental and a truly moral tending at its end to become a spiritual law of action and the fruits of action of Karma.

Mind Nature and Law of Karma

Man is not after all in the essence of his manhood or in the inner reality of his soul a vital and physical being raised to a certain power of mental will and intelligence. If that were so, the creed that makes our existence a manifestation of a Will to life, a Life Force moved by no other object than its own play, heightening, efficient power, expansion, might have a good chance of being the sufficient theory of our universe, and the law of our Karma, the rule of our activities would be in entire consonance with that one purpose and ordered by that dominant principle. Certainly in a great part of this world's outer activities, — or if we, fixing our eye mainly on the vital play of the spirit of the universe, consider them as man's chief business and the main thing that matters, — there is a colourable justification for this limited view of the human being. But the more he looks into himself and the more he goes inward and lives intimately and preeminently in his mind and soul, the more he discovers that he is in his essential nature a mental being encased in body and emmeshed in the life activities, *manu*, *manomaya puruṣa*. He is more than a thinking, willing and feeling result of the mechanism of the physical or an understanding nexus of the vital forces. There is a mental energy of his being that overtops, pervades and utilises the terrestrial action and his own terrestrial nature.

This character of man's being prevents us from resting satisfied with the vitalistic law of Karma: the lines of the vital energy are interfered with and uplifted and altered for man by the intervention of the awakened mental energy of the spirit that emerges in the material universe and creates here on earth the form of man for its habitation, his complex nature to be its expressive power, the gamut of its music, and the action of his thought, perception, will, emotions the notation of its harmonies. The apparent inconscience of physical Nature, the beautiful and terrible, kindly and cruel conscious but amoral Life Force that is the first thing we see before us, are not the whole self-expression of the universal Being here and therefore not the whole of Nature. Man comes into it to express and realise a higher law of Nature and therefore a higher system of the lines of Karma. The mental energy divides itself and runs in many directions, has an ascending scale of the levels of its action, a great variety and combination of its dynamic aims and purposes. There are many strands of its weaving and it follows each along its own line and combines manifoldly the threads of one with the threads of another. There is in it an energy of thought that puts itself out for a return and a constant increase of knowledge, an energy of will that casts itself forth for a return and increase of conscious mastery, fulfilment of the being, execution of will in action, an energy of conscious aesthesis that feels out for a return and an increase of the creation and enjoyment of beauty, an energy of emotion that demands in its action a return and a constant increase of the enjoyment and satisfaction of the emotional power of the being. All these energies act in a way for themselves and yet depend upon and are inextricably accompanied and mingled with each other. At the same time mind has descended into matter and has to act in and through this world of the vital and physical energy and to consent to and make something of the lines of the vital and physical Karma.

Man, then, since he is a mental being, a means of the evolution of the mental self-expression of the spirit, cannot confine the rule of his action and nature to an obedience to the vital and physical law and an intelligent utilisation of it for the greater, more ordered, more perfect enjoyment of his vital and physical existence, perpetuation, reproduction, possession, enjoyment, expansion. There is a higher law of mental being and nature of which he is bound to become aware and to seek to impose it on his life and his action. At first he is very predominantly governed by the life needs and the movement of the life energies, and it is in applying his mental energy to them and to the world around him that he makes the earliest development of his powers of knowledge and will and trains the crude impulses that lead him into the path of his emotional, aesthetic and moral evolution. But always there is a certain obscure element that takes pleasure in the action of the mental energies for their own sake and it is this, however imperfect at first in self-consciousness and intelligence, that represents the characteristic intention of Nature in him and makes his mental and eventually his spiritual evolution inevitable. The insistence of the external world around him and the need of utilising its opportunities and of meeting its siege and dangers causes his mind to be much obsessed by life and external action and the utility of thought and will and perception for his dealings with the physical and life forces, and to this preoccupation the finer more disinterested action and subtler cast of motive of the mind nature demanding its own inner development, seeking for knowledge, mastery, beauty, a purer emotional delight for their own sake, and the pursuits which are characteristic of this higher energy of the mental nature, appear almost as by-products and at any rate things secondary that can always be postponed and made subordinate to the needs and demands of the mentalised vital and physical being. But the finer and more developed mind in humanity has always turned towards an opposite self-seeing, inclined to regard this as the most characteristic and valuable element of our being and been ready to sacrifice much and sometimes all to its calls or its imperative mandate. Then life itself would be in reality for man only a field of action for the evolution, the opportunity of new experience, the condition of difficult effort and mastery of the mental and spiritual being. What then will be the lines of this mental energy and how will they affect and be affected by the lines of the vital and physical Karma?

Three movements of the mental energy of man projecting itself along the lines of life, successive movements that yet overlap and enter into each other, have created a triple strand of the law of his Karma. The first is that, primary, obvious, universal, predominant in his beginnings, in which his mind subjects and assimilates itself to the law of life in matter in order to make the most of the terrestrial existence for its own pleasure and profit, *artha*, *kāma*, without any other modification or correction of its pre-existing lines than is involved in the very impact of the human intelligence, will, emotion, aesthesis. These indeed are forces that lift up and greatly enlarge and infinitely rarify and subtilise by a consciously regulated and more and more skilful and curious use the first crude, narrow and essentially animal aims and movements common to all living creatures. And this element of the mentalised vital existence, these lines of its movement making the main grey solid stuff of the life of the average economic, political, social, domestic man may take on a great amplitude and an imposing brilliance, but they remain always in their distinctive, their original and still persistent character the lines of movement, the way of Karma of the thinking, willing, feeling, refining human animal, — not to be despised or excluded from our total way of being when we climb to a higher plane of conception and action, but still only a small part of human possibility and, if regarded as the main preoccupation or most imperative law of the human being, then limiting and degrading it; for, empowered up to a certain point to enlarge and dynamise and enrich, but not raise to a veritable self-exceeding, they are useful for ascension only when themselves uplifted and transformed by a greater law and a nobler motive. The momentum of this energy may be a very powerful mental action, may involve much output of intelligence and will power and aesthetic perception and expenditure of emotional force, but the return it seeks is vital success and enjoyment and possession and satisfaction. The mind no doubt feeds its powers on the effort and its fullness on the prize, but it is tethered to its pasture. It is a mixed movement, mental in its means, predominantly vital in its returns; its standard of the values of the return are measured by an outward success and failure, an externalised or externally caused pleasure and suffering, good fortune and evil fortune, the fate of the life and the body. It is this powerful vital preoccupation which has given us one element of the current notion of law of Karma, its idea of an award of vital happiness and suffering as the measure of cosmic justice.

The second movement of mind running on the lines of life comes into prominent action when man evolves out of his experience the idea of a mental rule, standard, ideal, a concretised abstraction which is suggested at first by life experience, but goes beyond, transcends the actual needs and demands of the vital energy and returns upon it to impose some ideal mental rule, some canon embodying a generalised conception of Right on the law of life. For its essence is the discovery or belief of the mind that in all things there is a right rule, a right standard, a right way of thought, will, feeling, perception, action other than that of the intuition of vital nature, other than that of the first dealings of mind seeking only to profit by the vital nature with a mainly vital motive, — for it has discovered a way of the reason, a rule of the self-governing intelligence. This brings into the seeking of vital pleasure and profit, *artha, kāma,* the power of the conception of a mental truth, justice, right, the conception of Dharma. The greater practical part of the Dharma is ethical, it is the idea of the moral law. The first mind movement is non-moral or not at all characteristically moral, has only, if at all, the conception of a standard of action justified by custom, the received rule of life and therefore right, or a morality indistinguishable from expediency, accepted and enforced because it was found necessary or helpful to efficiency, power, success, to victory, honour, approval, good fortune. The idea of Dharma is on the contrary predominantly moral in its essence. Dharma on its heights holds up the moral law in its own right and for its own sake to human acceptance and observance. The larger idea of Dharma is indeed a conception of the true law of all energies and includes a conscience, a rectitude in all things, a right law of thought and knowledge, of aesthesis, of all other human activities and not only of our ethical action. But yet in the notion of Dharma the ethical element has tended always to predominate and even to monopolise the concept of Right which man creates, — because ethics is concerned with action of life and his dealing with his vital being and with his fellow men and that is always his first preoccupation and his most tangible difficulty, and because here first and most pressingly the desires, interests, instincts of the vital being find themselves cast into a sharp and very successful conflict with the ideal of Right and the demand of the higher law. Right ethical action comes therefore to seem to man at this stage the one thing binding upon him among the many standards raised by the mind, the moral claim the one categorical imperative, the moral law the whole of his Dharma.

At first however the moral conceptions of man and the direction and output and the demand of return of the ethical energy in him get themselves inextricably mixed with his vital conceptions and demands and even afterwards lean on them very commonly and very considerably for a support and incentive. Human morality first takes up an enormous mass of customary rules of action, a conventional and traditional practice much of which is of a very doubtful moral value, gives to it an imperative sanction of right and slips into the crude mass or superimposes on it, but still as a part of one common and equal code, the true things of the ethical ideal. It appeals to the vital being, his desires, hopes and fears, incites man to virtue by the hope of rewards and the dread of punishment, imitating in this device the method of his crude and fumbling social practice: for that, finding its law and rule which, good or bad, it wishes to make imperative as supposing it to be at least the best calculated for the order and efficiency of the community, opposed by man's vital being, bribes and terrifies as well as influences, educates and persuades him to acceptance. Morality tells man, accommodating itself to his imperfection, mostly through the mouth of religion, that the moral law is imperative in itself, but also that it is very expedient for him personally to follow it, righteousness in the end the safest policy, virtue the best paymaster in the long run, — for this is a world of Law or a world ruled by a just and virtuous or at least virtue-loving God. He is assured that the righteous man shall prosper and the wicked perish and that the paths of virtue lie through pleasant places. Or, if this will not serve, since it is palpably false in experience and even man cannot always deceive himself, it offers him a security of vital rewards denied here but conceded in some hereafter. Heaven and hell, happiness and suffering in other lives are put before him as the bribe and the menace. He is told, the better to satisfy his easily satisfied intellect, that the world is governed by an ethical law which determines the measure of his earthly fortunes, that a justice reigns and this is justice, that every action has its exact rebound and his good shall bring him good and his evil evil. It is these notions, this idea of the moral law, of righteousness and justice as a thing in itself imperative, but still needing to be enforced by bribe and menace on our human nature, — which would seem to show that at least for that nature they are not altogether imperative, — this insistence on reward and punishment because morality struggling with our first unregenerate being has to figure very largely as a mass of restraints and prohibitions and these cannot be enforced without some fact or appearance of a compelling or inducing outward sanction, this diplomatic compromise or effort at equivalence between the impersonal ethical and the personal egoistic demand, this marriage of convenience between right and vital utility, virtue and desire, — it is these accommodations that are embodied in the current notions of the law of Karma.

What real truth is there behind the current notions of Karma in the actual facts or the fundamental powers of the life of man here or the visible working of the law of the energies of the cosmos? There is evidently a substantial truth, but it is a part only of the whole; its reign or predominance belongs to a certain element only, to the emphasis of one line among many of a transitional movement between the law of the vital energy and a greater and higher law of the mind and spirit. A mixture of any two kinds of energy sets up a mixed and complex action of the output of the energy and the return, and a too sharp-cut rule affixing vital returns to a mental and moral output of force is open to much exception and it cannot be the whole inner truth of the matter. But still where the demand is for the vital return, for success, an outer happiness, good, fortune, that is a sign of the dominant intention in the energy and points to a balance of forces weighing in the indicated direction. At first sight, if success is the desideratum, it is not clear what morality has to say in the affair, since we see in most things that it is a right understanding and intelligent or intuitive practice of the means and conditions and an insistent power of the will, a settled drive of the force of the being of which success is the natural consequence. Man may impose by a system of punishments a check on the egoistic will and intelligence in pursuit of its vital ends, may create a number of moral conditions for the world's prizes, but this might appear, as is indeed contended in certain vitalistic theories, an artificial imposition on Nature and a dulling and impoverishment of the free and powerful play of the mind force and the life force in their alliance. But in truth the greatest force for success is a right concentration of energy, *tapasyā*, and there is an inevitable moral element in Tapasya.

Man is a mental being seeking to establish a control over the life forces he embodies or uses, and one condition of that mastery is a necessary self-control, a restraint, an order, a discipline imposed on his mental, vital and physical being. The animal life is automatically subjected to certain measures; it is the field of an instinctive vital Dharma. Man, liberated from these automatic checks by the free play of his mind, has to replace them by willed and intelligent restraints, an understanding measure, a voluntary discipline. Not only a powerful expenditure and free play of his energies, but also a right measure, restraint and control of them is the condition of his life's success and soundness. The moral is not the sole element: it is not entirely true that the moral right always prevails or that where there is the dharma, on that side is the victory. The immediate success often goes to other powers, even an ultimate conquest of the Right comes usually by an association with some form of Might. But still there is always a moral element among the many factors of individual and collective or national success and a disregard of acknowledged right has at some time or other disastrous or fatal reactions. Moreover, man in the use of his energies has to take account of his fellows and the aid and opposition of their energies, and his relations with them impose on him checks, demands and conditions which have or evolve a moral significance. There is laid on him almost from the first a number of obligations even in the pursuit of vital success and satisfaction which become a first empirical basis of an ethical order.

And there are cosmic as well as human forces that respond to this balance of the mental and moral and the vital order. First there is something subtle, inscrutable and formidable that meets us in our paths, a Force of which the ancient Greeks took much notice, a Power that is on the watch for man in his effort at enlargement, possession and enjoyments and seems hostile and opposite. The Greeks figured it as the jealousy of the gods or as Doom, Necessity, Ate. The egoistic force in man may proceed far in its victory and triumph, but it has to be wary or it will find this power there on the watch for any flaw in his strength or action, any sufficient opportunity for his defeat and downfall. It dogs his endeavour with obstacle and reverse and takes advantage of his imperfections, often dallying with him, giving him long rope, delaying and abiding its time, — and not only of his moral short-comings but of his errors of will and intelligence, his excesses and deficiencies of strength and prudence, all defects of his nature. It seems overcome by his energies of Tapasya, but it waits its season. It overshadows unbroken or extreme prosperity and often sur-prises it with a sudden turn to ruin. It induces a security, a self-forgetfulness, a pride and insolence of success and victory and leads on its victim to dash himself against the hidden seat of justice or the wall of an invisible measure. It is as fatal to a blind self-righteousness and the arrogations of an egoistic virtue as to vicious excess and selfish violence. It appears to demand of man and of individual men and nations that they shall keep within a limit and a measure, while all beyond that brings danger; and therefore the Greeks held moderation in all things to be the greatest part of virtue.

There is here something in the life forces obscure to us, considered by our partial feelings sinister because it crosses our desires, but obedient to some law and intention of the universal mind, the universal reason or Logos which the ancients perceived at work in the cosmos. Its presence, when felt by the cruder kind of religious mind, generates the idea of calamity as a punishment for sin, — not observing that it has a punishment too for ignorance, for error, stupidity, weakness, defect of will and tapasya. This is really a resistance of the Infinite acting through life against the claim of the imperfect ego of man to enlarge itself, possess, enjoy and have, while remaining imperfect, a perfect and enduring happiness and complete felicity of its world-experience. The claim is, we may say, immoral, and the Force that resists it and returns, however uncertainly and late to our eyes, suffering and failure as a reply to our imperfections, may be considered a moral Force, an agent of a just Karma, though not solely in the narrowly ethical sense of Karma. The law it represents is that our imperfections shall have their passing or their fatal consequences, that a flaw in our output of energy may be mended or counterbalanced and reduced in consequence, but if persisted in shall react even in excess of its apparent merits, that an error may seem to destroy all the result of the Tapasya, because it springs from a radical unsoundness in the intention of the will, the heart, the ethical sense or the reason. This is the first line of the transitional law of Karma.

A second line of Karmic response of the cosmic forces to our action puts on also an appearance which tempts us to give it a moral character. For there can be distinguished in Nature a certain element of the law of the talion or — perhaps a more appropriate figure, since this action seems rather mechanical than rational and deliberate — a boomerang movement of energy returning upon its transmitter. The stone we throw is flung back by some hidden force in the world life upon ourselves, the action we put out upon others recoils, not always by a direct reaction, but often by devious and unconnected routes, on our own lives and sometimes, though that is by no means a common rule, in its own exact figure or measure. This is a phenomenon so striking to our imagination and impressive to our moral sense and vital feelings that it has received some kind of solemn form and utterance in the thought of all cultures, — "What thou hast done, thou must suffer", "He that uses the sword shall perish by the sword;" "Thou hast sown the wind and thou shalt reap the whirlwind;" — and we are tempted to erect it into a universal rule and accept it as sufficient evidence of a moral order. But the careful thinker will pause long before he hastens to subscribe to any such conclusion, for there is much that militates against it and this kind of definite reaction is rather exceptional than an ordinary rule of human life. If it were a regular feature, men would soon learn the code of the draconic impersonal legislator and know what to avoid and the list of life's prohibitions and vetoes. But there is no such clear penal legislation of Nature.

The mathematical precision of physical Nature's action and reaction cannot indeed be expected from mental and vital Nature. For not only does everything become infinitely more subtle, complex and variable as we rise in the scale so that in our life action there is an extraordinary intertwining of forces and mixture of many values, but, even, the psychological and moral value of the same action differs in different cases, according to the circumstance, the conditions, the motive and mind of the doer. The law of the talion is no just or ethical rule when applied by man to men and, applied by superhuman dispenser of justice or impersonal law with a rude rule of thumb to the delicate and intricate tangle of man's life action and life motives, it would be no better. And it is evident too that the slow, long and subtle purposes of the universal Power working in the human race would be defeated rather than served by any universality of this too precise and summary procedure. Accordingly we find that its working is occasional and intermittent rather than regular, variable and to our minds capricious rather than automatic and plainly intelligible.

At times in the individual's life the rebound of this kind of Karma is decisively, often terribly clear and penal justice is done, although it may come to him in an unexpected fashion, long delayed and from strange quarters; but however satisfactory to our dramatic sense, this is not the common method of retributive Nature. Her ways are more tortuous, subtle, unobtrusive and indecipherable. Often it is a nation that pays in this way for past crimes and mistakes and the sign manual of the law of the talion is there to point the lesson, but individually it is the innocent who suffer. A commercially minded king of Belgium is moved to make a good thing of the nation's rubber estate and human cattle farm in Africa and his agents murder and mutilate and immolate thousands of cheap negro lives to hasten the yield and swell his coffers. This able monarch dies in the splendour of riches and the sacred odour of good fortune, his agents in no way suffer: but here of a sudden comes Germany trampling her armed way towards a dream of military and commercial empire through prosperous

Belgium and massacred men and women and mutilated children startlingly remind us of Karma and illustrate some obscure and capricious law of the talion. Here at least the nation in its corporate being was guilty of complicity, but at other times neither guilty individual nor nation is the payer, but perhaps some well-meaning virtuous blunderer gets the account of evil recompense that should have been paid in of rights by the strong despots before him who went on their way to the end rejoicing in power and splendour and pleasure.

It is evident that we cannot make much of a force that works out in so strange a fashion, however occasionally striking and dramatic its pointing at cause and consequence. It is too uncertain in its infliction of penalty to serve the end which the human mind expects from a system of penal justice, too inscrutably variable in its incidence to act as an indicator to that element in the human temperament which waits upon expediency and regulates its steps by a prudential eye to consequence. Men and nations continue to act always in the same fashion regardless of this occasional breaking out of the lightnings of a retaliatory doom, these occasional precisions of Karmic justice amidst the uncertainties of the complex measures of the universe. It works really not on the mind and will of man — except to some degree in a subtle and imperfect fashion on the subconscient mind — but outside him as a partial check and regulator helping to maintain the balance of the returns of energy and the life purposes of the world-spirit. Its action is like that of the first line of transitional Karma intended to prevent the success of the vital egoism of man and serves as an interim compression and compulsion until he can discover and succeed in spite of his vital self in obeying a higher law of his being and a purer dynamism of motive in his directing mind and governing spirit. It serves therefore a certain moral purpose in the will in the universe, but is not itself, even in combination with the other, sufficient to be the law of a moral order.

A third possible and less outwardly mechanical line of Karma is suggested by the dictum that like creates like and in accordance with that law good must create good and evil must create evil. In the terms of a moral return or rather repayment to moral energies this would mean that by putting forth love we get a return of love and by putting forth hatred a return of hatred, that if we are merciful or just to others, others also will be to us just or merciful and that generally good done by us to our fellow-men will return in a recompense of good done by them in kind and posted back to our address duly registered in the moral post office of the administrative government of the universe. Do unto others as you would be done by, because then they will indeed so do to you, seems to be the formula of this moral device. If this were true, human life might indeed settle down into a very symmetrical system of a harmoniously moral egoism and a mercantile traffic in goodness that might seem fair and beautiful enough to those who are afflicted with that kind of moral aesthesis. Happily for the upward progress of the human soul, the rule breaks down in practice, the world-spirit having greater ends before it and a greater law to realise. The rule is true to a certain extent in tendency and works sometimes well enough and the prudential intelligence of man takes some account of it in action but it is not true all the way and all the time. It is evident enough that hatred, violence, injustice are likely to create an answering hatred, violence and injustice and that I can only indulge these propensities with impunity if I am sufficiently powerful to defy resistance or so long as I am at once strong enough and prudent enough to provide against their natural reactions. It is true also that by doing good and kindness I create a certain goodwill in others and can rely under ordinary or favourable circumstances not so much on gratitude and return in kind as on their support and favour. But this good and this evil are both of them movements of the ego and on the mixed egoism of human nature there can be no safe or positive reliance. An egoistic selfish strength, if it knows what to do and where to stop, even a certain measure of violence and injustice, if it is strong and skilful, cunning, fraud, many kinds of evil, do actually pay in man's dealing with man hardly less than in the animal's with the animal, and on the other hand the doer of good who counts on a return or reward finds himself as often as not disappointed of his bargained recompense. The weakness of human nature worships the power that tramples on it, does homage to successful strength, can return to every kind of strong or skilful imposition belief, acceptance, obedience: it can crouch and fawn and admire even amidst movements of hatred and terror; it has singular loyalties and unreasoning instincts. And its disloyalties too are as unreasoning or light and fickle: it takes just dealing and beneficence as its right and forgets or cares not to repay. And there is worse; for justice, mercy, beneficence, kindness are often enough rewarded by their opposites and ill will an answer to goodwill is a brutally common experience. If something in the world and in man returns good for good and evil for evil, it as often returns evil for good and, with or without a conscious moral intention, good for evil. And even an unegoistic virtue or a divine good and love entering the world awakens hostile reactions. Attila and Jenghiz on the throne to the end, Christ on the cross and Socrates drinking his portion of hemlock are no very clear evidence for any optimistic notion of a law of moral return in the world of human nature.

There is little more sign of its sure existence in the world measures. Actually in the cosmic dispensation evil comes out of good and good out of evil and there seems to be no exact correspondence between the moral and the vital measures. All that we can say is that good done tends to increase the sum and total power of good in the world and the greater this grows the greater is likely to be the sum of human happiness and that evil done tends to increase the sum and total power of evil in the world and the greater this grows, the greater is likely to be the sum of human suffering and, eventually, man or nation doing evil has in some way to pay for it, but not often in any intelligibly graded or apportioned measure and not always in clearly translating terms of vital good fortune and ill fortune.

In short, what we may call the transitional lines of Karma exist and have to be taken into account in our view of the action of the world forces. But they are not and cannot be the whole law of Karma. And they cannot be that because they are transitional, because good and evil are moral and not vital values and have a clear right only to a moral and not a vital return, because reward and punishment put forward as the conditions of good doing and evil doing do not constitute and cannot create a really moral order, the principle itself, whatever temporary end it serves, being fundamentally immoral from the higher point of view of a true and pure ethics, and because there are other forces that count and have their right, — knowledge, power and many others. The correspondence of moral and vital good is a demand of the human ego and like many others of its demands answers to certain tendencies in the world mind, but is not its whole law or highest purpose. A moral order there can be, but it is in ourselves and for its own sake

that we have to create it and, only when we have so created it and
found its right relation to other powers of life, can we hope to
make it count at its full value in the right ordering of man's vital
existence.

THE HIGHER LINES OF KARMA

The Higher Lines of Karma

The third movement of mind labours to bring the soul of man out of the tangle of the vital and mental forces and opens to him a field in which the mind raises itself, raises at least the head of its thought and will, above the vital demands and standards and there at that top of its activities, whatever its other concessions to the lower Karma, lives for the sake of the true values, the true demands of a mental being, even though one imprisoned in a body and set to wrestle with the conditions of life in a material universe. The innate demand of the mental being is for mental experience, for the mind's manifold strengths, its capacities, joys, growth, perfections, and for these things for their own sake because of the inevitable satisfaction they give to his nature, — the demand of the intellect for truth and knowledge, the demand of the ethical mind for right and good, the demand of the aesthetic mind for beauty and delight of beauty, the demand of the emotional mind for love and the joy of relation with our fellow-beings, the demand of the will for self-mastery and mastery of things and the world and our existence. And the values which the mental being holds for supreme and effective are the values of truth and knowledge, of right and good, of beauty and aesthetic delight, of love and emotional joy, of mastery and inner lordship. It is these things that he seeks to know and follow, to possess, discover, enjoy, increase. It is for this great adventure that he came into the world, to walk hardily through the endless fields they offer to him, to experiment, to dare, to test the utmost limit of each capacity and follow each possibility and its clue to the end as well as to observe in each its at present discovered law and measure. Here as in the other fields, as in the vital and physical, so in his mental provinces, it is the appointed work of his intelligence and will to know and master through an always enlarging experience the conditions of an increasing light and power and right and truth and joy and beauty and wideness, and not only to discover the Truth and the Law and set up a system and an order, but to enlarge continually its lines and boundaries. And therefore in these fields, as in life, man, the mental being, cannot stop short too long in the partial truth of an established system and a temporary mistaken for an eternal order — here least, because as he advances he is always tempted still farther forward until he realises that he is a seeker of the infinite and a power of the absolute. His base here plunges into the obscure infinite of life and matter; but his head rises towards the luminous infinite of the spirit.

The third movement of the mental energy carries it therefore into its own native field and kingdom above the pressing subjection to the lowering and limiting claim of a vital and physical Karma. It is true that his lower being remains subject to the law of life and of the body, and it is true also that he must strive either to find in life or to bring into the world around him some law of truth, of right and good, of beauty, of love and joy, of the mind's will and mastery, for it is by that effort that he is man and not the animal and without it he cannot find his true satisfaction in living. But two things he has more and more to feel and to realise, first, that life and matter follow their own law and not, in man's sense of it at least, a moral, a rational, a mentally determined aesthetic or other mind order, and if he wishes to introduce any such thing into them, he must himself here create it, transcending the physical and the vital law and discovering another and a better, and secondly, that the more he follows these things for their own sake, the more he discovers their true form, *svarūpa*, and develops their force to prevail upon and lift up life into an air of higher nature. In other words he passes from the practical pursuit of a serviceable knowledge, morality, aesthesis, force of emotion and will-power, — serviceable for his vital aims, for life as it first is, — to an ideal pursuit of these things and the transformation of life into the image of his ideal. This he is unable indeed as yet to realise and is obliged to rest on balance and compromise, because he has not found the whole reconciling secret of that which lies beyond his ideals. But it is as he pursues them in their purity, for their own imperative innate demand and attraction, on the line of their trend to their own infinite and absolute that he gets nearer in his total experience to the secret. There is so a chance of his discovering that as the beauty and irrefragable order of life and matter are due to the joy of the Infinite in life and in matter and the fidelity of the Force here at work to the hidden knowledge and will and idea of the Self and Spirit in them, so there is within his own hidden self, his own vast and covert spirit a secret of the Infinite's self-knowledge, will, joy, love and delight, mastery, right and truth of joy and action by which his own greater life rising above the vital and mental limitations can discover an infinite perfection and beauty and delight in itself and spontaneous irrefragable order.

Meanwhile this third movement of mind discovers a law of the return of mental energies, pure in its kind and as certain as the vital and the physical, as faithful to itself, to the self of mind and to mind nature, a law not of vital returns to mental dynamis, but of progression of the soul in the being and force of good and beauty and power — of mind-power and soul-power — and greatness and love and joy and knowledge. Mounting here the ethical mind no longer follows good for a reward now on earth or in another existence, but for the sake of good, and no longer shuns evil for fear of punishment on earth later on in this life or else in another life or in hell, but because to follow evil is a degradation and affliction of its being and a fall from its innate and imperative endeavour. This is to it a necessity of its moral nature, a truly categorical imperative, a call that in the total more complex nature of man may be dulled or suppressed or excluded by the claim of its other parts and their needs, but to the ethical mind is binding and absolute. The virtue that demands a reward for acting well and needs a penalty to keep it walking in the straight way, is no real portion, no true law of the ethical being, but rather a mixed creation, a rule of his practical reason that seeks always after utility and holds that to be right which is helpful and expedient, a rule that looks first not at the growth of the soul but at the mechanical securing of a regulated outward conduct and to secure it bribes and terrifies the vital being into acquiescence and a reluctant subordination of its own instincts and natural ventures. The virtue so created is an expediency, a social decency, a prudent limitation of egoism, a commercial substitute for the true thing; or, at best, it is a habit of the mind and not a truth of the soul, and in the mind a fabrication, mixed and of inferior stuff, a conventional virtue, insecure, destructible by the wear and tear of life, easily confused with other expediencies or purchasable or conquerable by them, — it is not a high and clear upbuilding, an enduring and inwardly living self-creation of the soul. Whatever its practical utility or service as a step of the transition, the mental habit of confusion and vitalistic compromise it fosters and the more questionable confusions and compromises that habit favours, have made conventional morality one of the chief of the forces that hold back human life from progressing to a true ethical order. If humanity has made any lasting and true advance, it has been not through the virtue created by reward and punishment or any of the sanctions powerful on the little vital ego, but by an insistence from the higher mind on the lower, an insistence on right for its own sake, on imperative moral values, on an absolute law and truth of ethical being and ethical conduct that must be obeyed whatever the recalcitrances of the lower mind, whatever the pains of the vital problem, whatever the external result, the inferior issue.

This higher mind holds its pure and complete sway only on a few high souls, in others it acts upon the lower and outer mind but amidst much misprision, confusion and distortion of thought and will and perverting or abating mixture; on the mass of men governed by the lower egoistic, vital and conventional standards of conduct its influence is indirect and little. None the less it gives the clue we have to follow in order to pursue the spiral ascent of the lines of Karma. And first we observe that the just man follows the ethical law for its own sake and not for any other purpose whatsoever, is just for the sake of justice, righteous for the sake of righteousness, compassionate for the sake of compassion, true for the sake of truth alone. Harishchandra sacrificing self and wife and child and kingdom and subjects in an unswerving fidelity to the truth of the spoken word, Shivi giving his flesh to the hawk rather than fall from his kingly duty of protection to the fugitive, the Bodhisattwa laying his body before the famished tiger, images in which sacred or epic legend has consecrated this greater kind of virtue, illuminate an elevation of the ethical will and a law of moral energy that asks for no return from man or living thing or from the gods of Karma, lays down no conditions, makes no calculation of consequence, of less or more or of the greatest good of the greatest number, admits neither the hedonistic nor the utilitarian measure, but does simply the act as the thing to be done because it is right and virtue and therefore the very law of being of the ethical man, the categorical imperative of his nature.

This kind of high absoluteness in the ethical demand is appalling to the flesh and the ego, for it admits of no comfortable indulgence and compromise, no abating reserves or conditions, no profitable compact between the egoistic life and virtue. It is offensive too to the practical reason, for it ignores the complexity of the world and of human nature and seems to savour of an extremism and exclusive exaggeration as dangerous to life as it is exalted in ideal purpose. *Fiat justitia ruat coelum*, let justice and right be done though the heavens fall, is a rule of conduct that only the ideal mind can accept with equanimity or the ideal life tolerate in practice. And even to the larger ideal mind this absoluteness becomes untrustworthy if it is an obedience not to the higher law of the soul, but to an outward moral law, a code of conduct. For then in place of a lifting enthusiasm we have the rigidity of the Pharisee, a puritan fierceness or narrowness or the life-killing tyranny of a single insufficient side of the nature. This is not yet that higher mental movement, but a straining towards it, an attempt to rise above the transitional law and the vitalistic compromise. And it brings with it an artificiality, a tension, a coercion, often a repellent austerity which, disregarding as it does sanity and large wisdom and the simple naturalness of the true ethical mind and the flexibilities of life, tyrannising over but not transforming it, is not the higher perfection of our nature. But still even here there is the feeling out after a great return to the output of moral energy, an attempt well worth making, if the aim can indeed so be accomplished, to build up by the insistence on a rigid obedience to a law of moral action that which is yet non-existent or imperfectly existent in us but which alone can make the law of our conduct a thing true and living, — an ethical being with an in-alienably ethical nature. No rule imposed on him from outside, whether in the name of a supposed mechanical or impersonal law or of God or prophet, can be, as such, true or right or binding on man: it becomes that only when it answers to some demand or aids some evolution of his inner being. And when that inner being is revealed, evolved, at each moment naturally active, simply and spontaneously imperative, then we get the true, the inner and intuitive Law in its light of self-knowledge, its beauty of self-fulfilment, its intimate life significance. An act of justice, truth, love, compassion, purity, sacrifice becomes then the faultless expression, the natural outflowering of our soul of justice, our soul of truth, our soul of love and compassion, our soul of purity or sacrifice. And before the greatness of its imperative mandate to the outer nature the vital being and the practical reason and surface seeking intelligence must and do bow down as before something greater than themselves, something that belongs directly to the divine and the infinite.

Meanwhile we get the clue to the higher law of Karma, of the output and returns of energy, and see it immediately and directly to be, what all law of Karma, really and ultimately, if at first covertly, is for man, a law of his spiritual evolution. The true return to the act of virtue, to the ethically right output of his energy—his reward, if you will, and the sole recompense on which he has a right to insist,—is its return upon him in a growth of the moral strength within him, an upbuilding of his ethical being, a flowering of the soul of right, justice, love, compassion, purity, truth, strength, courage, self-giving that he seeks to be. The true return to the act of evil, to the ethically wrong output of energy—his punishment, if you will, and the sole penalty he has any need or right to fear,—is its return upon him in a retardation of the growth, a demolition of the upbuilding, an obscuration, tarnishing, impoverishing of the soul, of the pure, strong and luminous being that he is striving to be. An inner happiness he may gain by his act, the calm, peace, satisfaction of the soul fulfilled in right, or an inner calamity, the suffering, disturbance, unease and malady of its descent or failure, but he can demand from God or moral Law no other. The ethical soul,—not the counterfeit but the real,—accepts the pains and sufferings and difficulties and fierce intimidations of life, not as a punishment for its sins, but as an opportunity and trial, an opportunity for its growth, a trial of its built or native strength, and good fortune and all outer success not as a coveted reward of virtue, but as an opportunity also and an even greater more difficult trial. What to this high seeker of Right can mean the vital law of Karma or what can its gods do to him that he can fear or long for? The ethical-vitalistic explanation of the world and its meaning and measures has for such a soul, for man at this height of his evolution no significance. He has travelled beyond the jurisdiction of the Powers of the middle air, the head of his spirit's endeavour is lifted above the dull grey-white belt that is their empire.

There can be no greater error than to suppose, misled by this absolute insistence of the ethical being, that the ethical is the single or the supreme demand of the Infinite upon us or the one law and line of the higher Karma, and that in comparison with it nothing else matters. The German thinker's idea that there is a categorical imperative laid upon man to seek after the right and good, an insistent law of right conduct, but no categorical imperative of the

Oversoul compelling him to seek after the beautiful or the true, after a law of right beauty and harmony and right knowledge, is a singular misprision. It is a false deduction born of too much preoccupation with the transitional movement of man's mind and, there too, only with one side of its complex phenomena. The Indian thinkers had a wiser sight who while conceding right ethical being and conduct as a first need, still considered knowledge to be the greater ultimate demand, the indispensable condition, and much nearer to a full seeing came that larger experience of theirs that either through an urge towards absolute knowledge or a pure impersonality of the will or an ecstasy of divine love and absolute delight, — and even through an absorbing concentration of the psychical and the vital and physical being, — the soul turns towards the Supreme and that on each part of our self and nature and consciousness there can come a call and irresistible attraction of the Divine. Indeed, an uplift of all these, an imperative of the Divine upon all the ways of our being, is the impetus of self-enlargement to a complete, an integralising possession of God, freedom and immortality, and that therefore is the highest law of our nature.

The fundamental movement of life knows nothing of an absolute ethical insistence, its only categorical imperative is the imperative of Nature herself compelling each being to affirm its life as it must or as best it can according to its own inborn self and way of expression of her, Swabhava. In the transitional movement of life informed by mind there is indeed a moral instinct developing into a moral sense and idea, — not complete for it leaves large ranges of conduct in which there is a lacuna or inconscience of the moral sense, a satisfied fulfilment of the egoistic desires at the expense of others, and not imperative since it is easily combated and overthrown by the earlier imposed, more naturally dominant law of the vital being. What the natural egoistic man obeys most rigorously is the collective or social rule of conduct impressed on his mind by law and tradition, *jus, mores,* and outside its conventional circle he allows himself an easy latitude. The reason generalises the idea of a moral law carrying with it an obligation man should heed and obey but may disregard at this outer or that inner peril, and it insists first and most on a moral law, an obligation of self-control, justice, righteousness, conduct, rather than a law of truth, beauty and harmony, love, mastery, because the regulation of his desires and instincts and his outward vital action is his first necessary preoccupation and he has to find his poise here and a settled and sanctioned order before he commences securely to go deeper and develop more in the direction of his inner being. It is the ideal mind that brings into this superficial moral sense, this relative obligation, the intuition of an inner and absolute ethical imperative, and if it tends to give to ethics the first and most important and in some minds the whole place, it is still because the priority of action, long given to it in the evolution of mind on earth, moves man to apply first his idealism to action and his relations with other beings. But as there is the moral instinct in the mind seeking for good, so too there is the aesthetic instinct, the emotional and the dynamic and the instinct in man that seeks after knowledge, and the developing reason is as much concerned to evolve in all these directions as in the ethical and to find out their right law; for truth, beauty, love, strength and power are after all as necessary for the true growth of mind and of life and even for the fullness of the action as righteousness, purity and justice. Arriving on the high ideal plane these too become, no less than the ethical motive, no longer a seeking and necessity of this relative nature and importance, but a law and call to spiritual perfection, an inner and absolute divine imperative.

The higher mind of man seeks not only after good, but after truth, after knowledge. He has an intellectual as well as an ethical being and the impulse that moves it, the will to know, the thirst for truth is not less divine in its upward orientation than the will to good, not less too in its earlier workings, but even more, a necessity of the growth of our consciousness and being and the right ordering of our action, not less an imperative need laid upon man by the will of the spirit in the universe. And in the pursuit of knowledge as in the pursuit of good we see the same lines and stages of the evolution of energy. At first as its basis there is simply a life-consciousness seeking for its self, becoming more and more aware of its movements, actions and reactions, its environment, its habits, its fixed laws, gaining and enlarging and learning always to profit by self-experience. This is indeed the fundamental purpose of consciousness and use of intelligence, and intelligence with the thinking will in it is man's master faculty and supports and embraces, changes with its change and widens with its widening and increasingly perfects all the others. Mind in its first action pursues knowledge with a certain curiosity, but turns it mainly to practical experience, to a help that enables it to fulfil better and to increase more assuredly the first uses and purposes of life. Afterwards it evolves a freer use of the intelligence, but there is still a dominant turn towards the vital purpose. And we may observe that as a power for the returns of life the world energy seems to attach a more direct importance and give more tangible results to knowledge, to the right practical workings of the intelligence than it yields to moral right. In this material world it is at least doubtful how far moral good is repaid by vital good and moral evil punished by a recoil, but it is certain that we do pay very usually for our errors, for stupidity, for ignorance of the right way of action, for any ignoring or misapplication of the laws that govern our psychical, vital and physical being; it is certain that knowledge is a power for life efficiency and success. Intelligence pays its way in the material world, guards itself against vital and physical suffering, secures its vital rewards more surely than moral right and ethical purpose.

But the higher mind of humanity is no more content with a utilitarian use of knowledge as its last word in the seeking of the intelligence than with a vitalistic and utilitarian turn and demand of the ethical being. As in the ethical, so in the intellectual being of man there emerges a necessity of knowledge which is no longer its utility for life, its need of knowing rightly in order to act rightly, to deal successfully and intelligently with the world around it, but a necessity of the soul, an imperative demand of the inner being. The pursuit of knowledge for the sake of knowledge is the true, the intrinsic dharma of the intellect and not for the sake primarily or even necessarily at all for the securing or the enlargement of the means of life and success in action. The vital kinetic man tends indeed to regard this passion of the intellect as a respectable but still rather unpractical and often trivial curiosity: as he values ethics for its social effects or for its rewards in life, so he values knowledge for its external helpfulness; science is great in his eyes because of its inventions, its increase of comforts and means and appliances: his standard in all things is vital efficiency. But in fact Nature sees and stirs from the first to a larger and more inward Will and is moved with a greater purpose, and all seeking for knowledge springs from a necessity of the mind, a necessity of its nature, and that means a necessity of the soul that is here in nature. Its need to know is one with its need to grow, and from the eager curiosity of the child upward to the serious stress of mind of the thinker, scholar, scientist, philosopher the fundamental purpose of Nature, the constant in it, is the same. All the time that she seems busy only with the maintenance of her works, with life, with the outward, her secret underlying purpose is other,—it is the evolution of that which is hidden within her: for if her first dynamic word is life, her greater revealing word is consciousness and the evolution of life and action only the means of the evolution of the consciousness involved in life, the imprisoned soul, the Jiva. Action is a means, but knowledge is the sign and the growth of the conscious soul is the purpose. Man's use of the intelligence for the pursuit of knowledge is therefore that which distinguishes him most from other beings and gives him his high peculiar place in the scale of existence. His passion for knowledge, first world-knowledge, but afterwards self-knowledge and that in which both meet and find their common secret, God-knowledge, is the central drift of his ideal mind and a greater imperative of his being than that of action, though later in laying its complete hold on him, greater in the wideness of its reach and greater too in its effectiveness upon action, in the returns of the world energy to his power of the truth within him.

It is in the third movement of highest mind when it is preparing to disengage itself, its pure self of will and intelligence, the radiant head of its endeavour from subjection to the vital motive that this imperative of nature, this intrinsic need that creates in the mind of man the urge towards knowledge, becomes something much greater, becomes instead more and more plainly the ideal absolute imperative of the soul emerging from the husks and sheaths of ignorance and pushing towards the truth, towards the light as the condition of its fulfilment and the very call of the Divine upon its being. The lure of an external utility ceases to be at all needed as an incentive towards knowledge, just as the lure of a vital reward offered now or hereafter ceases on the same high level of our ascent to be needed as an incentive to virtue, and to attach importance to it under whatever specious colour is even felt to be a degradation of the disinterestedness, a fall from the high purity of the soul motive. Already even in the more outward forms of intellectual seeking something of this absoluteness begins to be felt and to reign. The scientist pursues his discoveries in order that he may know the law and truth of the process of the universe and their practical results are only a secondary motive of the enquiring mind and no motive at all to the higher scientific intelligence. The philosopher is driven from within to search for the ultimate truth of things for the one sake of Truth only and all else but to see the very face of Truth becomes to him, to his absorbing mind and soul of knowledge, secondary or of no importance; nothing can be allowed to interfere with that one imperative. And there is the tendency to the same kind of exclusiveness in the interest and the process of this absolute. The thinker is concerned to seek out and enforce the truth on himself and the world regardless of any effect it may have in disturbing the established bases of life, religion, ethics, society, regardless of any other consideration whatsoever: he must express the word of the Truth whatever its dynamic results on life. And this absolute becomes most absolute, this imperative most imperative when the inner action surpasses the strong coldness of intellectual search and becomes a fiery striving for truth experience, a luminous inner truth living, a birth into a new truth consciousness. The enamoured of light, the sage, the Yogin of knowledge, the seer, the Rishi live for knowledge and in knowledge, because it is the absolute of light and truth that they seek after and its claim on them is single and absolute.

At the same time this also is a line of the world energy, — for the world Shakti is a Shakti of consciousness and knowledge and not only a Power of force and action, — and the output of the energy of knowledge brings its results as surely as the energy of the will seeking after success in action or after right ethical conduct. But the result that it brings on this higher plane of the seeking in mind is simply and purely the upward growth of the soul in light and truth; that and whatever happiness it brings is the one supreme reward demanded by the soul of knowledge and the darkening of the light within, the pain of the fall from truth, the pain of the imperfection of not living only by its law and wholly in the light is its one penalty of suffering. The outward rewards and the sufferings of life are small things to the higher soul of knowledge in man: even his high mind of knowledge will often . face all that the world can do to afflict it, just as it is ready to make all manner of sacrifices in the pursuit and the affirmation of the truth it knows and lives for. Bruno burning in the Roman fire, the martyrs of all religions suffering and welcoming as witnesses to the light within them torture and persecution, Buddha leaving all to discover the dark cause of universal suffering in this world of the impermanence and the way of escape into the supreme Permanence, the ascetic casting away as an illusion life in the world and its activities, enjoyments, attractions with the one will to enter into the absolute truth and the supreme consciousness are witnesses to this imperative of knowledge, its extreme examples and exponents.

The intention of Nature, the spiritual justification of her ways appears at last in this turn of her energies leading the conscious soul along the lines of truth and knowledge. At first she is physical Nature building her firm field according to a base of settled truth and law but determined by a subconscient knowledge she does not yet share with her creatures. Next she is Life growing slowly self-conscious, seeking out knowledge that she may move seeingly in them along her ways and increase at once the complexity and the efficacy of her movements, but developing slowly too the consciousness that knowledge must be pursued for a higher and purer end, for truth, for the satisfaction, as the life expression and as the spiritual self-finding of the soul of knowledge. But, last, it is that soul itself growing in the truth and light, growing into the absolute truth of itself which is its perfection, that becomes the law and high end of her energies. And at each stage she gives returns according to the development of the aim and consciousness of the being. At first there is the return of skill and effectual intelligence — and her own need explains sufficiently why she gives the rewards of life not, as the ethical mind in us would have it, to the just, not chiefly to moral good, but to the skilful and to the strong, to will and force and intelligence, — and then, more and more clearly disengaged, the return of enlightenment and the satisfaction of the mind and the soul in the conscious use and wise direction of its powers and capacities and, last of all, the one supreme return, the increase of the soul in light, the satisfaction of its perfection in knowledge, its birth into the highest consciousness and the pure fulfilment of its own innate imperative. It is that growth, a divine birth or spiritual self-exceeding its supreme reward, which for the eastern mind has been always the highest gain, — the growth out of human ignorance into divine self-knowledge.

APPENDIX I
The Tangle of Karma

If the idea or the knowledge we have arrived at in our dealings with the higher lines of Karma be the right illumining idea and the clear highest knowledge in this matter or even if it be at all near to the true truth of things, obviously we must leave far behind us the current theory of Karma and its shallow attempt to justify the ways of the Cosmic Spirit by forcing on them an identity with the notions of law and justice and reward and punishment dear to the surface human mind. There is here a more authentic and spiritual truth at the base of Nature's action and a far less mechanically calculable movement. No rigid narrow ethical law bound down to a petty human significance is here, no unprofitable wheel of a brutal cosmic justice automatically moved in the traces of man's ignorant judgments and earthy desires and instincts. Not these artificial constructions but a thing spiritual and intimate to the deepest intention of Nature. The ascending march of the soul's consciousness and experience as it emerges out of subconscient Matter and climbs to its own luminous divinity fixes the norm and constantly enlarges the lines of the law or let us say rather since law is too mechanical a conception the truth of Karma.

For what we understand by law is an habitual movement or recurrence in Nature fruitful of a determined sequence of things that must be always clear, precise, limited to its formula, invariable. If it is not that, if there is too much flexibility, variety of movement, too rich a complex of forces, then it seems to the narrow uncompromising incompetence of our logical mind not law but an incertitude and a chaos. Our reason must be allowed to cut and hew and arbitrarily select its circumstances, isolate immutable data and anatomise and skeletonise or at least mechanise life if it is at all to think or act. We must deal with Nature just as we try to build and map out our own artificial laws of society, politics, ethics, conduct in a clear precise rigid infallible system and leave as little room as possible for the infinite flexibility and variability and complexity that presses from the Infinite upon our mind and life. Now this thing we call Karma seems to turn out after all to be no such precise and limited and invariable mechanism as we hoped, but rather a thing of many planes and spirals of movement and in each plane even we find not one movement but an indefinite complex of many movements hard enough for us to harmonise together or to find out whatever secret harmony now unknown to us and incalculable these complexities are weaving out in this mighty field of the dealings of the soul with Nature. Let us then call Karma no longer a Law, but rather the many-sided dynamic truth of action and life, the organic movement here of the Infinite. That was what the ancient thinkers saw in it before it was cut out into an easy and popular and misleading formula. Action of Karma follows and takes up into its flexible sweep and surge many potential lines of the Spirit; it is the processus of the creative Infinite; it is the long and many-sided way of the progression of the individual and the cosmic soul in Nature. Its complexities cannot be unravelled by our physical mind ever bound up in the superficial appearance, nor by our vital mind of desire stumbling forward in the cloud of its own longings and instincts and rash determinations through the maze of the myriad favouring and opposing forces of the visible and the invisible worlds. Nor can it be perfectly classified, accounted for, tied up in bundles by the precisions of our logical intelligence in its inveterate search for clear-cut formulas. On that day only shall we perfectly decipher what now to us is Nature's obscure hieroglyph of Karma when there rises in us that supramental way of knowledge which can see a hundred meeting and diverging motions in one glance and envelop in the largeness of its harmonising vision of Truth all that to us now is clash and opposition and the collision and interlocked strife of numberless contending forces. For truth to the supramental sight is at once single and infinite and the complexities of its play bring out miraculously and with an abundant ease the rich significance of its many-sided oneness.

The complexity of the lines of Karma is much greater than we have yet seen in the steps of thought that we have been obliged to cut in order to climb to the summits where they converge. For the convenience of the mind we have chosen to speak as if there were four quite separate planes each with its separate lines of Karma, — the physical with its fixed law and very easily perceptible return to our energies, the life plane, complex, full of doubtful rewards and dangerous rebounds, rich promise and dark menace, the mind plane with its high trenchant unattainable absolutes each in its separateness so difficult to embody and all so hard to reconcile and combine and the supramental where Nature's absolutes are reached, her relativities ordered to their place and all the lower movements delivered and harmonised luminously because they have found their inner spiritual reason for existence. That division is not false in itself, but its truth is subject to two capital provisos which at once give them a complexity not apparent in the first formula. There are above and behind our human existence these four levels but there each plane contains in itself the others, although in each these others are subject to the dominant law of the plane, — life for instance obeys on the mental level the law of mind and turns its movements into an instrumentation of the free intelligence. Again man exists here in the body and the physical world; he is open more or less to the vast movements of a life plane and the free movements of a mental world that are far vaster and freer in their potentialities than anything that we call here life and mind, but he does not live in that free mental light or in that vast vital force. His business is to bring down and embody here as much of that greater life and greater mind as can be precipitated into matter and equipped with a form and organised in the physical formula. In proportion as he ascends he does indeed rise above the physical and vital into the higher mental lines of Karma, but he cannot leave them entirely behind him. The saint, the intellectual man, scientist, thinker or creator, the seeker after beauty, the seeker after any mental absolute is not that alone; he is also, even if less exclusively than others the vital and physical man; subject to the urgings of the life and the body, he participates in the vital and physical motives of Karma and receives the perplexed and intertwined return of these energies. It is not intended in his birth that he shall live entirely in mind, for he is here to deal with life and Matter as well and to bring as best he can a higher law into life and Matter. And since he is not a mental being in a mental world, it is not easy and in the end, we may suspect not possible for him to impose entirely and perfectly the law of the mental absolutes, — mental good, beauty, love, truth and power on his lower parts. He has to take this other difficult truth into account that life and Matter have absolutes of their own armed with an equal right to formulation and persistence and he has to find some light, some truth, some spiritual and supramental power that can take up these

imperatives also no less than the mind's imperatives and harmonise all in a grand and integral transformation. But the difficulty is
again that if he is not open to the world of free intelligence, he is
still less open to the deeper and vaster spiritual and supramental
levels. There can indeed be great descents of spiritual light, purity,
power, love, delight into the earth consciousness in its human
formula; but man as he is now can hold only a little of these things
and he can give them no adequate organisation and shape and
body in his mental movements or his life-action or his physical and
material consciousness and dynamis. The moment he tries to get at
the absolute of the spirit, he feels himself obliged to reject body, to
silence mind, and to draw back from life. It is that urgent
necessity, that inability of mind and life and body to hold and
answer to the spirit that is the secret of asceticism, the philosophical justification of the illusionist, the compulsion that moves
the eremite and the recluse. If on the other hand he tries to
spiritualise mind and life and the body he finds in the end that he
has only brought down the spirit to a lower formulation that
cannot give all its truth and purity and power. He has to some
extent spiritualised mind, but much more has he mentalised the
spiritual and to mentalise the spiritual is to falsify and obscure it or
at the very least to dilute its truth, to imprison its force, to limit
and alter its potentialities. He has perhaps to a much less extent
spiritualised his life, but much more has he vitalised the spiritual
and to vitalise the spiritual is to degrade it. He has never yet
spiritualised the body, at most he has minimised the physical by a
spiritual refusal and abstinence or brought down some mental and
vital powers mistaken for spiritual into his physical force and
physical frame. More has not been done in the human past so far
as we can discover, or if anything greater was done it was a
transitory gain from the superconscient and has returned again
into our superconscience.

The secret reason of man's failure to rise truly beyond himself
is a fundamental incapacity in the mind, the life and the body to
organise the highest integral truth and power of the spirit. And this
incapacity exists because mind and life and matter are in their
nature depressed and imperfect powers of the Infinite that need to
be transformed into something greater than themselves before
they can escape from their depression and imperfection; in their
very nature they are a system of partial and separated values and

cannot adequately express or embody the integral and the one, a movement of many divergent and mutually non-understanding or misunderstanding lines they cannot arrive of themselves at any but a provisional limited and imperfect harmony and order. There is no doubt a material Infinite, a vital Infinite, a mental Infinite in which we feel a perfection, a delight, an essential harmony, an inexpressible completeness which, when we experience it, makes us disregard the discords and imperfections and obscurities we see and even perceive them as elements of the infinite perfection. In other words the Spirit, the Infinite, supports these depressed values and elicits from them a certain joy of his manifestation that is complete and illimitable enough in its own manner. But there is more behind and above, there are greater more unmistakably harmonious values, greater truly perfect powers of the Spirit than mind, life and matter and these wait for their expression and only when they are expressed can we escape from this system of harmony through discords and of a perfection in the whole that subsists by imperfection in the detail. And as we open to a greater knowledge, we find that even for such harmonies, stabilities, perfections as the energies of Mind, Life and Matter can realise, they depend really not on their own delegated and inferior power which is at best a more or less ignorant instrument but on a greater deeper organising force and knowledge of which they are the inadequate derivations. That force and knowledge is the self-possessed supramental power and will and the perfect and un-trammelled supramental gnosis of the Infinite. It is that which has fixed the precise measures of Matter, regulates the motive instincts and impulsions of Life, holds together the myriad seekings of Mind; but none of these things are that power and gnosis and nothing therefore mental, vital or physical is final or can even find its own integral truth and harmony nor all these together their reconciliation until they are taken up and transformed in a supramental manifestation. For this supermind or gnosis is the entire organising will and knowledge of the spiritual, it is the Truth Consciousness, the Truth Force, the organic instrumentation of divine Law, the all-seeing eye of the divine Vision, the freely selecting and generating harmony of the eternal Ananda.

APPENDIX II

(The question of a sadhak with Sri Aurobindo's reply)

Q: In Chapter II, "The Reincarnating Soul", of "Rebirth and Karma" it is stated:

"We have in fact an immutable Self, a real Person, lord of this ever-changing personality which, again, assumes ever-changing bodies, but the real Self knows itself always as above the mutation, watches and enjoys it, but is not involved in it. Through what does it enjoy the changes and feel them to be its own, even while knowing itself to be unaffected by them? The mind and ego-sense are only inferior instruments; there must be some more essential form of itself which the Real Man puts forth, puts in front of itself, as it were, and at the back of the changings to support and mirror them without being actually changed by them. This more essential form is or seems to be in man the mental being or mental person which the Upanishads speak of as the mental leader of the life and body, *manomayaḥ prāṇa-śarīra-netā*. It is that which maintains the ego-sense as a function in the mind and enables us to have the firm conception of continuous identity in Time as opposed to the timeless identity of the Self."[1]

In this passage I find that it is "the mental being" which is put forth from life to life and that it is the reincarnating soul. But would not the mental being be a part of the personality—the mental, nervous and physical composite—which in the popular conception is the thing that is carried over or which takes a new body in next life? And the "Self" in this passage is quite different from "the mental being"—that means the mental being is yet another kind of "self". Is "the mental being" then the same as "the psychic being" which is carried over to the next life?

A: The mental being spoken of by the Upanishad is not part of the mental nervous physical composite—it is the *manomayaḥ puruṣaḥ prāṇa-śarīra-netā*, the mental being leader of the life and body. It could not be so described if it were part of the composite. Nor can the composite or part of it be the Purusha,—for the composite is composed of Prakriti. It is described as *manomaya* by the Upanishads because the psychic being is behind the veil and man being the mental being in the life and body lives in his mind

[1] Page 17.

and not in his psychic, so to him the *manomaya puruṣa* is the leader of the life and body, — of the psychic behind supporting the whole he is not aware or dimly aware in his best moments. The psychic is represented in man by the Prime Minister, the *manomaya*, itself being a mild constitutional king; it is the *manomaya* to whom Prakriti refers for assent to her actions. But still the statement of the Upanishads gives only the apparent truth of the matter, valid for man and the human stage only — for in the animal it would be rather the *prāṇamaya puruṣa* that is the *netā*, leader of mind and body. It is one reason why I have not yet allowed the publication of Rebirth and Karma because this had to be corrected and the deeper truth put in its place. I had intended to do it later on, but had not the time to finish the remaining articles.

24 December 1935

Editor's Note

The essays that make up this book were first published in the monthly journal *Arya* between 1915 and 1921, as follows:

The last instalment appeared in the last issue of *Arya* to be published.

Sometime in the 1920s Sri Aurobindo revised the *Arya* essays and had most of them printed in the form of a book that was to be entitled *The Problem of Rebirth*. (This title has been used for all editions of the book published in India. In this American edition the more descriptive title *Rebirth and Karma* has been used.) The revision of the 1920s included the addition of three long passages: a paragraph at the end of "The Significance of Rebirth", three paragraphs at the end of "Involution and Evolution" and three paragraphs at the end of "Karma, Will and Consequence". For some reason the printing of this revised edition was never completed and the book was never released. In a letter of 1935 (printed in its entirety in Appendix II) Sri Aurobindo wrote that he had "not yet allowed the publication of Rebirth and Karma" because a certain viewpoint "had to be corrected and the deeper truth put in its place." He "had intended to do it later on, but had not the time to finish the remaining articles." The essay printed as Appendix I seems to be a draft for one of the proposed additional articles. It was written along with several incomplete drafts in or about 1927. (One of the incomplete drafts was published on pages 33-35 of Volume 17 of the *Sri Aurobindo Birth*

Centenary Library. This draft bears the title "The Tangle of Karma", which has been borrowed by the editors for the piece published here as Appendix I.)

In 1952, two years after Sri Aurobindo's passing, the first edition of *The Problem of Rebirth* was brought out. The editors of this edition divided the essays into three sections and incorporated most of the verbal revisions that Sri Aurobindo had made in the 1920s. A second edition of the book was brought out in 1969 and reprinted in 1973. This edition was textually identical to the first and included as an appendix the letter quoted from above along with the question that had elicited it. A third edition, reproduced photographically from the *Sri Aurobindo Birth Centenary Library* text, was published in 1978. This incorporated for the first time a number of minor textual changes and additions by the author, including one footnote. It also included as an appendix a version of "The Tangle of Karma" that differs in some respects from the version reproduced in the present edition. The 1978 edition was reproduced in 1983 and 1987.

The text of the present edition, the first to be published in the United States, is identical to that of the fourth Indian edition, the only difference being the change of title. The text has been carefully checked against Sri Aurobindo's manuscripts. Following indications left in the unpublished edition of the 1920s, the editors have arranged the essays in two rather than three sections. Sri Aurobindo in fact left no section divisions as such, though he did place the last essays under the rubric "The Lines of Karma." (In *Arya* the last instalment, "The Lines of Truth", was placed under the rubric "The Higher Lines of Karma". Later Sri Aurobindo incorporated this instalment in the essay entitled "The Higher Lines of Karma".) Editorial emendations and alternative versions have been listed in the Table of Emendations and Variants. Sanskrit and Greek words have been transliterated according to the systems generally used in Sri Aurobindo's works. Such words are not listed in the Table.

Table of Emendations and Variants

Page	Line	Text	Former text
5	23	overhang	over hang
6	3	exact, profuse	exact profuse
6	7	than	then
6	fn	This was written in pre-Einsteinian [*MS:* "Eynsteinian"] days.	[*variant:*] This was written before the appearance of the theories of Einstein[.][1]
7	23	those	these
7	26	make-up	makeup
9	5	governed.	governed?
9	24	tacking . . . to the deeper	[*variant:*] taking [*typographical error*] . . . and gluing them to the deeper
10	5	huckster	hucksterer
19	5	body,	body;
24	22	matter.	matter,
42	19	seem	seems
47	36	*brahma*	*Brahma*
51	30	kinds	kind
54	19	sorcerer's	sorceror's
61	39	system.	system,
65	28	variations,	variations
75	21	ate	eat
75	fn	Upanishad.	Upanishad
80	11	sibyllic	sybillic
80	37	"might-have-been"s,	"might-have-beens,"
83	6	Man, too, may	Man, too may
90	1	someone	some one
96	9	*vistarasya*	*vistarya*
101	30	have it paid out	have it paid it out
114	4	to	the
120	9	steps,	steps
129	7	by-products	bye-products
139	6	an unegoistic	a unegoistic
155	6	an	a
155	15	Nature.	Nature
155	26	Our	our
155	29	act.	act
155	31	and	*cancelled without substitution*
156	2	and spirals	& spirals

[1] The two texts of this footnote were written independently in different versions. The editors have chosen the one that is more strictly correct. (Einstein's special theory of relativity was published in 1905, before *The Problem of Rebirth* was written, but did not become generally known for several years.)

156	14	many-sided	manysided
156	23	formulas.	formulas
156	31	the	its
156	32	oneness.	oneness
156	35	converge.	converge
156	39	full of	full
156	40	menace,	menace
157	10	each	Each
157	14	intelligence.	intelligence
157	36	parts.	parts
158	32	superconscience.	superconsicence.
158	34	mind,	mind
159	2	non-understanding	nonunderstanding
159	5	Infinite,	Infinite
159	10	Spirit,	Spirit
159	10	Infinite,	Infinite
159	13	behind	behind,
159	15	mind,	mind
159	19	that even	even that even
159	20	Mind,	Mind

Glossary of Sanskrit Terms

adhyāropa, imposition.

adṛṣṭa, Fate (the unseen thing).

aghaṭana-ghaṭana-paṭīyasī, very skillful in bringing about the impossible.

ānanda, bliss, delight, beatitude; a self-delight which is the very nature of the transcendent and infinite existence.

anumantā, giver of the sanction.

aṇur hyeṣa dharmaḥ, subtle is the law of it.

apraketaṁ salilaṁ sarvam idam, all this was an ocean of inconscience. (Rig Veda 10.129.3)

artha, interest; material, economic and other aims and needs of the mind and body.

asat, non-being.

asura, Titan; a hostile being of the mentalised vital world.

asya mahimānam, his greatness. (Mundaka Upanishad 3.1.2; Shwetashwatara Upanishad 4.7)

brahman, the Reality; the Eternal; the Absolute; the Spirit; the One besides whom there is no other.

brahma satyaṁ jagan mithyā, the Eternal (Brahman) is true, the world is a lie. (Vivekachudamani 20)

citti acitti, the Knowledge and the Ignorance.

dandramyamāṇaḥ andhena nīyamāno yathāndhaḥ, beating about like the blind led by the blind. (Cf. Katha Upanishad 1.2.5.)

deva, god.

devānāṁ dhruva-vratāni, the fixed laws of working of the gods.

dharma, law of being.

dhruvam adhruveṣu, permanence in things that pass. (Katha Upanishad 2.1.2)

divya janma, the divine birth.

ekaṁ bījaṁ bahudhā śakti-yogāt, one seed, manifold by the yoga of might.

gahanā karmaṇo gatiḥ, thick and tangled is the way of works. (Bhagavad Gita 4.17)

īśvara (Ishwara), Lord, Master.

jīva, the spirit individualised and upholding the living being in its evolution from birth to birth; individual self; central being.

kāma, desire.

karma, work, action; the principle of Action in the universe with its stream of cause and infallible effect—for man the sum of his past actions whose results reveal themselves not at once, but in the dispensation of Time, partly in this life, mostly in lives to come.

kṛpaṇāḥ phalahetavaḥ, poor and wretched souls are they who make the fruit of their works the object of their thoughts and activities.

laya,   dissolution.

mahimānam asya,   see *asya mahimānam*.

manomaya (puruṣa),   the mental Person, the mental being.

manomayaḥ (puruṣaḥ) prāṇa-śarīra-netā,   the mental Being, leader of the life and body. (Mundaka Upanishad 2.2.8)

manu,   the thinker, the mental being, man.

māyā,   phenomenal consciousness; signified originally in the Veda the comprehensive and creative knowledge, wisdom that is from old, afterwards taken in its second and derivative sense, cunning, magic, illusion.

mokṣa,   release, liberation.

mūlādhāra,   root vessel or chamber; the physical consciousness centre.

na karma lipyate nare,   action cleaves not to a man. (Isha Upanishad 2)

nāsti anto vistarasya me,   there is no end to My self-extension. (Bhagavad Gita 10.19)

netā,   leader.

nirvāṇa,   extinction (not necessarily of all being, but of being as we know it, extinction of ego, desire and egoistic action and mentality).

niyati,   Fate (the thing willed and executed by Nature according to a fixed law of its self-governed workings).

pariṇāma,   evolutionary change (out of the original substance of energy).

prakṛti (Prakriti),   executive or working force, Nature.

prakṛtir jīvabhūtā,   Nature which has become the *jīva*.

prāṇamaya puruṣa,   soul in life, the vital being.

punarjanma,   "again-birth", rebirth.

puṇya,   good, virtue, merit.

puruṣa (Purusha),   Person, Conscious-Being, Soul; essential being supporting the play of *prakṛti*.

puruṣaḥ purāṇaḥ sanātanaḥ,   ancient soul of long standing, sempiternal in being.

ṛtam,   Right, the truth of divine being regulating right activity both of mind and body.

śakti (Shakti),   Energy, Force, Strength, Will, Power; the self-existent, self-cognitive, self-effective Power of the Lord which expresses itself in the workings of *prakṛti*.

sambhava,   birth.

sambhūti,   becoming.

saṁhata,   combined.

sandhi,   joint, lock.

sāṅkhya,   the analysis, the enumeration and discriminative setting forth of the principles of our being (the name of one of the six systems of Indian philosophy).

sarvam idam,   all this.

sarvāṇi vijñāna-vijṛmbhitāni, all things are self-deployings of the Divine Knowledge.

śāśvatībhyaḥ samābhyaḥ, from years sempiternal.

satyam, truth of being.

Shakti, see *śakti.*

svabhāva (Swabhava), "own being"; the principle of self-becoming; essential nature and self-principle of being of each becoming; nature.

svadharma (Swadharma), own law of action; true rule and way of being.

svarūpa, self-form, essential form or figure.

tapas, the essential principle of energy; any kind of energism, askesis, austerity of conscious force acting upon itself or its object.

tapasas tan mahinā ajāyata ekam, that one was born by the greatness of his own energy. (Rig Veda 10.129.3)

tapasyā, effort, energism, austerity of the personal will.

tato na vicikitsate, he debates not thereafter.

vidyā avidyā, the Knowledge and the Ignorance.

Index

Other Titles by Sri Aurobindo:

Bases of Yoga	p	2.95
Essays on the Gita	p	16.50
Gems from Sri Aurobindo, 1st Series		
(Compiled)	p	8.95
Hidden Forces of Life (Compiled)	p	8.95
Hymns to the Mystic Fire	p	22.50
Isha Upanishad	p	3.95
The Life Divine	p	29.95
	hb	39.95
Lights on Yoga	p	2.95
Living Within (Compiled)	p	6.95
The Message of the Gita, with text (Compiled)	p	8.95
The Mother	p	1.50
A Practical Guide to Integral Yoga (Compiled)	p	7.95
The Problem of Rebirth (Rebirth and Karma)	p	7.95
The Psychic Being: Soul in Evolution		
(Compiled)	p	8.95
Savitri: A Legend and A Symbol	p	16.00
The Secret of the Veda	p	15.00
The Synthesis of Yoga	p	19.50
	hb	21.00
The Upanishads	p	16.50
Vedic Symbolism (Compiled)	p	6.95
Wisdom of the Upanishads (Compiled)	p	7.95

Available from your
Local Bookseller or:

LOTUS LIGHT PUBLICATIONS
P O Box 2, Wilmot, WI 53192 USA
414 862 2395